SpringerBriefs in Philosophy

Soraj Hongladarom

A Buddhist Theory of Privacy

Springer

Soraj Hongladarom
Department of Philosophy, Faculty of Arts
Chulalongkorn University
Bangkok
Thailand

ISSN 2211-4548 ISSN 2211-4556 (electronic)
SpringerBriefs in Philosophy
ISBN 978-981-10-0316-5 ISBN 978-981-10-0317-2 (eBook)
DOI 10.1007/978-981-10-0317-2

Library of Congress Control Number: 2015957799

Printed on acid-free paper

This Springer imprint is published by SpringerNature
The registered company is Springer Science+Business Media Singapore Pte Ltd.

Preface

This is a book about the philosophical underpinnings of privacy. However, what distinguishes it from most other books on the topic is that it is based on a Buddhist conception. The ideas in the book have had their beginnings in the articles that I have written before, but they are elaborated here in greater detail so it is not just a rehashing of the existing literature. Basically, this means that Buddhist insights serve as a foundation for a theory on privacy. Philosophically speaking, Buddhism is best known for its view that the self is ultimately non-existent, much like a rainbow is non-existent when observed up close. As information privacy is traditionally based on the idea that the individual has autonomy and dignity, which is argued from the view that there is a subsisting core to the individual, the book offers an alternative view that the foundation for privacy could be found on the radical idea that the individual does not have to be metaphysically self-subsistent, and accordingly privacy should be justified more on pragmatic grounds rather than metaphysical ones. Moreover, I also argue that this alternative view offers a more effective way to theorize about some newer forms of privacy that have emerged due to recent advances in technology, such as group privacy.

This short book has been long in the making. The first ideas were conceived back in 2007 and 2008 when I was engaged in a project of searching for a justification for the information privacy while preserving cultural identity. I received an opportunity to travel to Norway and Sweden in the winter of 2008 as an Erasmus Mundus exchange scholar, where I had a large extended period of free time during my teaching duties to start thinking seriously on the topic which eventually presented itself in this book. I would like to thank May Thorseth and Siri Granum Carson, who hosted me while I worked at the Norwegian University of Science and Technology in Trondheim in October 2008, and Göran Collste at Linköping University in Sweden, who hosted me while I moved from Trondheim to finish up the latter part of my stay as the Erasmus Mundus scholar in November of the same year. I would also like to thank Chulalongkorn University for granting me a sabbatical leave from October 2008 to September 2009, which enabled me the time to think more about the work and to do all the necessary research. After that the book got a long hiatus when I was engaged in other duties, and it is only in 2015 that I finally managed to put up a block of free time to push up this book to the shape it has taken at this moment.

The thanks would not be complete if I failed to acknowledge my debt to Charles Ess, who is both a friend and a colleague who kept pushing and challenging me to sharpen my ideas. We were interested in the topic of intercultural information ethics, and the conferences and seminars that he organized, especially the series of conferences on Cultural Attitude toward Technology and Communication (CATaC—http://www.catacconference.org/) played a very important role in my development as a scholar. My thanks also go to Rafael Capurro, who also gave me many opportunities to develop my research capabilities and critical thinking skills. Both Ess and Capurro are deeply interested in privacy and its cultural implications, the topic which develops itself into this book. I am deeply indebted to both of them.

Bangkok, Thailand
October 2015

Soraj Hongladarom

Contents

Chapter 1
Privacy in the World Today

Our societies, in the West and increasingly in the developing countries, are becoming saturated with technology. Let us imagine a day in a life of an ordinary person in such a society. He gets up from bed, and if he is a middle-class worker in Bangkok his bedroom will almost certainly be air-conditioned. Then he might log on his computer, which is always connected with the Internet through broadband network to check up morning news and his emails. Then he drives from his gated community from the outskirt of the city to work. He drives past the security post in front of his community, and his car is being observed and recorded through video surveillance in his community. Then he drives to work, stopping for gas. He uses his credit card to pay for it, and perhaps he does not know that his credit card number was submitted and recorded in the database of the bank in order to find out if he has had any bad credit records. Then when he entered his office, his entrance was recorded again by another system of video surveillance. He might enter his card into the employee system, recording the time of his arrival. He might even have to enter a set of numbers in order to enter the gate of his office.

Once he got to his room, he turned on his office computer again. There is a chance that his computer is being wired with the central server that records what kind of information passes through his computer; which websites he was watching; what keystrokes have been entered through his keyboard. He might buy something on the Internet, entering his credit card into the website, trusting that the seller does not abuse his number. Since he has bought something from this website before, the website has installed a cookie on his machine so that when he comes back the website knows his identity and his past purchase records. When he went back home, he orders a pizza for his family from the phone. But he is surprised to find out that once he gave the operator his phone number, she knew his name, his home address, and his pizza preferences. He wonders whether the pizza company knows more about him than what was told to him during the phone conversation. Furthermore, the devices in his home might be already talking to one another, and this includes also the devices on his body. His watch might be talking with his air-conditioner, for example, giving the status of his body temperature to the latter so that the latter could modify the ambient temperature in his room accordingly. The refrigerator might also be talking with the grocery store nearby so that when something is about to run out, the store will be notified and arrange the delivery on

S. Hongladarom, *A Buddhist Theory of Privacy*,
SpringerBriefs in Philosophy, DOI 10.1007/978-981-10-0317-2_1

time. If he has some medical conditions, the watch he is wearing and other devices he might have on his body could monitor his health at all times and communicate with his doctor. The possibilities are actually limitless.

Moreover, if he is a Thai citizen, he will be carrying the Thai national ID card. The card is equipped with a computer chip which contains information about his citizen ID number, his house registration and perhaps many other kinds of information. There is a concern that his citizen ID card might conceivably carry far more information than he knows about, information that could be a ground for a discrimination against those who happen to find themselves on the wrong side. For example, the ID card could possibly carry his health information, and as soon as he applies for a new insurance policy, the insurance company might have a link with the national database server and find out information about him that could put him in an unfavorable situation. Not only does his ID card contain digital information about himself, his passport is an "e-passport," meaning it also contains a chip, but one that is able to be read from a distance by a machine. So it is possible that wherever he goes, he always carries with himself all kinds of information about himself, broadcast everywhere for all who have the means to read it.

All these scenarios are not in some futuristic novel. It is already happening here and now. In Thailand, the use of national ID card with a computer chip, called smart ID card, is the norm, and practically every Thai citizen has a card like this in his or her pocket. And even in Thailand there is the talk of the Internet of things where household devices are part of the network. Thailand also has been issuing the electronic passport for many years now. These technological advances have penetrated even the developing country, and Thailand is certainly not alone. In its attempt to join in the world community and to engage with it in terms of commerce, information flow and many other things, Thailand has adopted many, if not all, the technological advances that have found themselves first in the developed economies. What is happening in Thailand is also happening elsewhere in the developing world. As countries scramble to integrate themselves into the globalized arena of trade, commerce, and information flow, the technologies that have arisen first in the developed countries eventually find themselves being used in other parts of the world too.

This has created a number of complicated problems. Concerns about the social, cultural, and ethical implications of these technologies have been around in the West for some time. These concerns naturally arise from the penetration and the saturation of technology into the people's daily lives. The scenario of a person whose personal data are being manipulated, systematized, categorized, and retrieved from huge population databases is commonplace in the West, but in the developing world this has just arisen. As the traditions and belief systems of the people in the developing world are not the same as those in the West, the concerns about ethical and social impacts are definitely not exactly identical. This is because in the developing world there is the added dimension where the technologies in question are not "home grown," so to speak. There are several problems with this. First of all, when the technology is not developed from within the cultural context where it is used, there is then the feeling that the technology is "alien" to the people who use it. When the technology is introduced into a non-Western country, it is usually transferred "wholesale" to the developing country without any clear understanding how the technology would fit in the cultural context or the value system of the country in question. This has created rather well-known problems, such as the people's alienated attitude toward technology, or their uncritical acceptance of technology driven by desire for immediate self gratification.

Second, in many cases the technology that is introduced seems to be only the prerogative of those who can afford it, and in many developing countries, the middle class and the market system is not well developed. Thus the people who can afford and who enjoy the technology are usually those who are in the position of power, or those who are close to those in power so they can enjoy the benefits the power could bring. In these cases, implications that follow the use of the technology, such as privacy, take a back seat to the sheer fact that the technology is being used. Thus there are many dimensions of inequality here. On the one hand, there is an inequality, or a "divide" between those in the developing country who are in the position of power and those who are not. On the other hand, the richer and more powerful groups in the developing world are contrasted from their counterparts in the West because they the latter group are more numerous relative to the general population whereas the rich and powerful in the developing country are much fewer in number. This results in the ethical issues that concern those in the West, such as privacy and personal data protection, are not perceived to be as serious. The issue seems to be rather the simple fact that the technology is being used at all and is being enjoyed by the powerful at the expense of the less fortunate.

Nonetheless, as the middle class continues to grow in these developing countries, the demand for the technology has skyrocketed. The demand for mobile phones in Thailand, for example, has risen dramatically in the last few years According to the figure released by the National Broadcasting and Telecommunication Commission, the level of penetration of the mobile phone in Thailand stood at close to 50 % in the year 2005, but in only 10 years it jumped to 139.25 % in 2015.[1] Hence, the ethical issues that have been the concerns of those in the West are increasingly being felt in the developing world too. This is compounded by the uses of advanced technology on the entire population, as in the case of the Thai citizen ID card. However, even if the ethical issues and other problems surrounding the use of technology might be familiar, the exact nature of the problems and how the problems and the ethical concerns are perceived and understood can be markedly different. That is, as Thailand and other developing countries are fast embracing the mobile Internet world, they have to face the same kind of ethical conundrums that have faced countries in the West. However, the way Thai culture sets about to solve these problems do not have to be exactly the same, as the traditions from which the attempt emerges are different. This is the

---

[1]The figure is obtained the website of the NBTC at http://www2.nbtc.go.th/TTID/mobile_market/penetration_postpre/.

reason why I propose to undertake a new way of approaching and theorizing the privacy problem from a Buddhist perspective.

*

These recent technological advances certainly call for a robust regulation on privacy to protect people's rights. However, privacy rights, as well as other values that are characteristic of the modern world, have been attacked as being Western values imposed the non-Western world. A familiar argument among those who follow this line is that people in the non-Western world have their own indigenous values that are different from those of the West. They can manage their lives well for millennia without following these Western values, so there is no reason why they should adopt them. The repeated calls by the West for people in other cultures to adopt these values are only a cover for power grabbing, now that overt colonialism is no longer acceptable. In other words, imposing Western values, such as calling for the world to adopt the same guidelines on informational privacy, is seen by some to be an aspect of the continuing attempt by the West to colonize the non-Western countries.[2] What I want to argue in this book is, however, precisely to counter this type of argument. It is true that people in the non-Western cultures should not adopt a set of foreign views and beliefs, no matter if they are forced to do so by superior weapons and technologies, or if they are "persuaded" to do so as a result of a process that Peter Hershock calls a "colonization of consciousness."[3] For Hershock, the fact that some members of a non-Western culture show a penchant toward Western values is that they have been led to believe in the superiority of these values without having an opportunity to examine them thoroughly and critically. Thus they are comparable to birds who have been raised in a cage and when the cage is open refuse to fly away. I also would like to combat Hershock's view in this book too.

Thus the point that I would like to argue for ultimately, through my examination of the Buddhist theory of privacy, is that people in non-Western cultures do not have to follow Western values, but that does not mean that they have to give up the rights and protection that some Western values, such as privacy (which is the topic of this book), afford. In fact this present book is both a continuation and a consolidation of my previous works on the topic of Buddhist conception and justification of privacy.[4] Countries such as Thailand, a typical non-Western country, are

---

[2]For example, the military junta that is controlling Thailand during the time of writing this chapter usually criticizes the West for "not understanding" the peculiarities of Thai political culture. The usual argument is that Thai culture has its unique identity which makes it unsuitable for Western-style democracy See "Transcript: Prayuth Chan-ocha," *Aljazeera,* 19 June 2015, available at http://www.aljazeera.com/programmes/talktojazeera/2015/06/transcript-prayuth-chan-ocha-150619102230894.html. For a collection of articles on the general debate on Asian values and the problem of universality, see *Sojourn: Journal of Social Issues in Southeast Asia*, Vol. 14, no. 2, October 1999, especially Raul Pertierra, "Introduction," which introduces the whole special volume.

[3]Hershock (1999).

[4]See Hongladarom (2007, 2008, 2009).

fast integrating itself with the global community. Thailand is a very good example in this regard because its economy is an integral part of the world's globalized economic system. It has stock markets; its currency is freely exchangeable with other currencies; Thai people are free to move around, and so on. Furthermore, a process is going on whereby the ten countries in the Association of Southeast Asian Nations (ASEAN) region will move toward an integration of their economies in a few years from now. This will only accelerate the process of integration with the world's economy. An important upshot is that this process of integration will result in rules and regulations having to be calibrated across all the participating countries. This, on the surface, appears to create a dilemma where on the one hand there is this process of globalization and on the other there is a need to protect one's cultural differences and identity, because many people are still strongly attached to their local traditions and their cultures. However, this attachment does not have to lead to an abandonment of globalization and refusal of Western values. In the case of privacy, this means that there should be a way to accept privacy as a value that is helpful in maintaining the dignity of individuals, while maintaining cultural and traditional identity. This means that, for a Buddhist country such as Thailand, there should be a way to integrate the teachings of Buddhism into how privacy should be understood and justified, without thereby modifying its content so much that it is no longer workable as a universal norm. I also argue that, by saying that privacy is a "universal norm" I do not intend to mean that it is based on the typically Western perspective of liberalism or on a theory derived from the Greeks' virtue ethics theory, or other Western theories; but I intend to say that the universality in privacy is there because privacy is recognized as one values in today's globalized information society which is indispensable if we are to maintain another deeper set of values that we in the modern world hold dear, such as democracy and respect for individuals. This is the core of my argument for a *pragmatic* conception of privacy, which, as I shall make clear in the book, has an intimate connection with Buddhist thought. Thus, in a nutshell, I am looking for a way for privacy to be theorized and justified in the vocabulary of a thoroughly non-Western philosophical system, while maintaining its efficacy for today's globalized world.

However, the Buddhist conception offered in this book is relevant not only to Thai people, but also to other members of non-Western cultures who can see and have a closer look at their intellectual traditions to find resources for their attempts to justify values such as privacy for their own purposes too. Moreover, this look back at one's own cultural resources does not mean that one completely accepts whatever the international guidelines or norms tell one to do. The look back to one's cultural resources does not necessarily imply any tacit or uncritical acceptance of the prevailing values of the time. On the contrary, the Buddhist conception, as well as other conceptions that could be later elaborated, such as the African conception of *ubuntu*, could perhaps be relevant to members of the Western culture and possibly to everyone concerned with how values such as privacy are to be justified. That is, by looking back at the Buddhist conception, one can also find from within Buddhism (and other intellectual or spiritual traditions) resources which could also shed a more critical light on how the prevailing values of the time should be understood and perhaps revised. No norms of this type, namely international guidelines that govern regulation of informational privacy, are written in stone, but they are more fluid and malleable than it appears. This fluidity of the norms shows that it is always subject to renegotiation by the international community. When the circumstances change, it is clear that the norms should change in order for the norms themselves to remain functional, relevant and effective. This means that, by looking closely at what Buddhism has to offer, everyone gains an insight into how an intellectual tradition which hitherto has been relatively neglected might be able to offer something new which could be relevant.

*

So this is the motivation for this short book. This is, basically speaking, a book about privacy and its philosophical justifications and theories according to the perspective of a non-Western culture, which here is represented mostly by Thai culture and Buddhism. There are already many excellent books and research articles on privacy. There are also even quite a lot of directly philosophical works on the issue. However, what most distinguishes this book from others, I believe, is that the book treats privacy from a perspective of a non-Western culture and belief system. There are a number of advantages in this, both for the readers in the West and outside. First, as the world is expanding rapidly and as globalization is becoming all pervasive, looking how advanced technology and indigenous cultures interact is extremely interesting because we can see how the culture adapts to the new technology and how technology itself is a function of its cultural context. Furthermore, ethical problems and how they are conceived and solved might not be the same in all cultures. This has an advantage because the West, for example, could learn from fresh insights brought into the pool of the global intellectual resources by the intellectual traditions of the non-West. Third, the people in the non-West, who are relative newcomers in dealing with advanced technology, would benefit from the book, I believe, through an analysis and a system of justification of privacy which takes into consideration their own intellectual tradition, which could reduce the problem of alienation alluded to earlier. Even though the book will rely rather extensively on the resources of Thai culture and Buddhism, this does not mean that those in other cultures in the developing world could not benefit, because they can readily adapt the insights here into their own cases.

The book is divided into four chapters. Chapter 2 deals with the philosophical foundations of privacy. Here the concept "privacy" will be analyzed and the various theories will be laid out to provide a background for the more elaborate and original treatment later on in the book. Privacy is a very difficult concept to pin down and precisely define. Nonetheless, the chapter will review how the major theories have defined the concept. The analysis of the concept will also lead to a discussion of privacy in relation with other important philosophical topics, such as autonomy (How is privacy related to individual autonomy?), privacy and justice (How could enforcement of privacy contribute to justice?), and the metaphysical problem of privacy and the individual (How is privacy possible under the metaphysical system which does not allow a full status of the individual?). The last question in particular is important because Buddhism presupposes this view of the individual as a construct, as something that does not exist on its own as a full metaphysical entity. This is in contrast with the standard liberal theory where normative guidelines on privacy rest on the notion of an autonomous individual. This very interesting topic, among the others, will be the subject matter of the second chapter.

Chapter 3 then discusses the cultural implications of privacy. As I have previously mentioned, the threat to privacy does not restrict itself only to the West, but as the technology is spreading to almost every corner of the globe, so is the threat. What is interesting is how the cultures of the world react to the issue. The chapter will then review some of the salient research on cultural responses to privacy. How does the Japanese culture, for example, deal with the issue of privacy? And what could the West learn from the Japanese in their responses to the technologies that could imperil their privacy, and what are their attitudes toward the problem? In a nutshell, then, the chapter will contain my philosophical reflections on this topic.

Chapter 4 is the heart of the book, as it outlines a Buddhist theory of privacy. Thus this will be the key chapter in the book. The attempt to ground a theory of privacy on Buddhism is that Buddhism does not recognize the full ontological status of the individual. Again, the force of the proposal in the chapter lies in the fact that it offers an alternative to the standard Western liberal notion that it is the autonomous individual that functions as the basis for privacy. For Buddhism, the status of the individual is that of a construction only. There is, metaphysically speaking, no such thing as an individual self. Thus there is the question of how a theory that is based on the idea that the self is nonexistent could itself ground such a practical concept as privacy. Answering this question will form the overall content of the chapter, and will provide a link to the pragmatic conception of privacy, which is closely linked to Buddhism. The pragmatic view I am proposing here is rather similar to a social constructivist one where normative statements are grounded upon social and other empirical factors. However, the difference is that the view is based on Buddhist teaching in the sense that the pragmatism is derived directly from Buddhist philosophy. The main idea that I am proposing in the chapter, and indeed in the book, is that privacy should be grounded, not on the metaphysical presupposition that the individual human being or the individual self fully exists as a subsistent metaphysical entity, but on the idea that, even though the individual is not a fully subsisting metaphysical entity (that is, the individual self is dependent on other factors for their subsisting as a functioning self), their privacy should still be maintained because doing so will promote a set of goals and values that are desirable and are conducive to certain ends. I call this a *pragmatic* conception of privacy. This idea, I believe, is relevant not only in the context of a Buddhist culture, but also elsewhere in Asia, where the dominant cultural context is that the individual does not exist as a fully subsistent metaphysical entity. The view could also benefit attempts to sustain privacy rights in the West too, as the emphasis is more on the link between privacy and democratic values rather than on justifying the former in isolation.

The Buddhist viewpoint on privacy will then form a basis for further reflections on the emerging concept of 'group privacy.' Traditionally privacy is thought to belong only to individuals. It has always seemed that only individuals do possess the quality of being private, and the protection of sensitive information has almost always centered on the individual. However, as today's "Big Data" technologies have become more sophisticated, it is now possible to collect information that belongs to groups of individuals in addition to that belonging to each individual alone.[5] It has now become possible, for example, to extract genetic information of a group of population who are close to one another genetically for a variety of purposes, such as to develop medicines that work specifically for those having particular genetic traits, or for a particular group of population. In other words, the chapter will deal with group privacy from a Buddhist viewpoint. (The Buddhist viewpoint I rely on in this book does not belong to any school in particular. Instead it is common to all Buddhist schools. I try consciously in this book not to go to doctrinal debates within Buddhism, which is an arcane matter and is not directly relevant to this book. Fortunately there is a set of tenets with which all Buddhist schools concur, and this will be the only basis for my Buddhist analysis in the book.) I will argue that the traditional way in which privacy is analyzed and justified does not seem to do enough justice to the emerging phenomenon of group privacy and the need to protect it as well as how the need is justified. The questions are: What exactly is group privacy? How is the concept going to be analyzed? Is there really such a thing, or is it just a collective way of characterizing the privacy of individuals considered together? The Buddhist viewpoint outlined in the previous chapter will figure prominently in my critique of the mainstream theories. Basically speaking, since Buddhism does not put emphasis on the metaphysical status of an individual self, then it becomes easier conceptually to delineate group privacy as a means toward a system of justification of the concept.

References

Hershock P (1999) Reinventing the wheel: a Buddhist response to the information age. SUNY Press, Albany

Hongladarom S (2007) Analysis and justification of privacy from a Buddhist perspective. In: Hongladarom S, Ess C (eds) Information technology Ethics: cultural perspectives. IGI Global, Hershey, pp 108–122

Hongladarom S (2008) Privacy, contingency, identity and the group. In: Luppicini R, Adell R (eds) Handbook of research on technoethics, vol. II IGI Global, Hershey, pp 496–511

Hongladarom S (2009) Privacy, the individual and genetic information: a Buddhist perspective. Bioethics 23(7):403–412

[5]For a discussion of big data in the context of ethics and metaphysics, see my "Big Data, Digital Traces and the Metaphysics of the Self," paper presented at the IACAP-CEPE Conference, University of Delaware, June 22–25, 2015.

Chapter 2
Philosophical Foundations of Privacy

Introduction

Compared with other topics, such as knowledge, democracy, or justice, privacy has received relatively less attention from philosophers. This is quite surprising, since privacy is an important concept and does play an important role in our lives. Compared to other topics in social philosophy such as equality, justice, or freedom, privacy seems to be a rather minor issue. Most academic literature on privacy come from law or communication studies, or the emerging field of Internet studies. Nonetheless, there are a number of very interesting philosophical works on the topic, and the purpose of this chapter is to review some of them.

In this chapter, then, I review what these philosophers have said about privacy, outlining, as it were, a conceptual map of privacy in order to find out what the terrains are and what connections there are to other topics. I start with the contentious problem of whether privacy, as a philosophical concept, is reducible to other, perhaps more fundamental ones. In an important anthology of philosophical analyses on the topic, Ferdinand Schoeman divides the debate into two main camps.[1] What he terms "the coherence thesis" states that there are underlying threads that actually connect talks and discourses about privacy together, and these threads are objective in the sense that they point to some really existing underlying issue. On the other hand, Schoemann calls the contrary position, the one denying that there are such underlying, objective threads, "the distinctiveness thesis." The first position holds that talks about privacy, since they are coherent with the other issues, are reducible to more fundamental concepts, while the distinctiveness position holds that discussions about privacy are not so reducible.

This is not surprising, since privacy is a very complicated concept. Though many have attempted to provide a definition, no clear consensus has actually emerged as to the official definition of privacy such that it is universally agreed. Thus, it is

---

[1] Schoemann (1984).

S. Hongladarom, *A Buddhist Theory of Privacy*,
SpringerBriefs in Philosophy, DOI 10.1007/978-981-10-0317-2_2

conceivable that when privacy is looked at through one perspective, then it appears to be reducible to other concepts, such as autonomy or integrity. On the other hand, when viewed differently, the concept appears to be irreducible. Judith Jarvis Thompson, for example, argues that there is no such thing as the right to privacy, since anything that is thought to be an instance of such a right could be explicated in terms of other concepts such as those related to the concepts of property or the person. For example, cutting someone's hair while she is asleep does not harm her, but her right is violated nonetheless, and that is the right over the person according to Thomson. In surreptitiously cutting her hair, her privacy is violated, so even though the act of cutting the hair does not cause bodily pain it is nonetheless a violation to her body. By thus violating her privacy, it is in fact her right over her own body that is violated. The basic idea, then, is that any putative instances of violation of the right to privacy turn out to be, on closer analysis, a violation of the right to person or the property.[2] On the other hand, Thomas Scanlon argues that there is indeed a common ground to the right of privacy, and that is the condition of "being able to be free from certain kinds of intrusions."[3] And it is the intrusions of our bodies, behaviors and interactions with others are some of the clear examples of intrusions that violate the norm of privacy.[4] Thus Scanlon would presumably argue that in cutting the hair of a person, the norm of privacy is violated in such a way that does not reduce to mere violation of the bodily integrity since the situation where one is free from intrusions such as cutting hair could be regarded as its own distinct category which is not one and the same as those of bodily harm or bodily integrity. In maintaining the privacy of one's own body, one has a certain amount of control over how one's body is perceived and is respected by others, and for Scanlon this constitutes the person's right to privacy in a way that does not reduce to the right to bodily integrity alone.

Even though privacy is closely related to other concepts, perhaps it would be beneficial if we maintained that privacy is a distinct concept and that discourses about privacy are not reducible to other topics. One benefit of doing this would be a clear idea of what one is actually doing when one discusses privacy in a variety of settings. For example, when one inserts a smart card into a machine, or when one carries an electronic passport equipped with an RFID chip, one's privacy would be threatened if the information related to the individual who carries the passport or who owns the card is used in a way that is not consented to by the individual in question. This could be reduced to some kind of bodily integrity, but in order for us to be able to focus our attention solely to the problem of information and of how such information is used, then a distinct concept of privacy seems to be in order. Furthermore, it is possible that no bodily harm is done but privacy is violated. In a case where a lover intentionally shows her body to her lover while she is taking a shower, no bodily harm seems to be done to her, yet her privacy is compromised

---

[2]Thomson (1975).

[3]Scanlon (1975).

[4]Thomas Scanlon, "Thomson on Privacy", p. 315.

even though she is always in control of how much her lover is allowed to see her body. The fact that she willingly opens up her body to her lover does not necessarily mean her privacy is kept intact. So perhaps there is a case to be made to distinguish bodily integrity or harm to the body or the right to the body from privacy.

*

In Roman times, the conception of "being private" had more to do with one's "private" domain where one is the master of one's own house rather than the sense we have today where the emphasis is more on one's private thoughts. According to the Merriam Webster Dictionary, the word *privacy* in English comes from Latin *privatus* which means "not in public life" (http://www.merriam-webster.com/dictionary/private). Another root of the word is *privus*, meaning "single, or alone." Hence the etymological root of the word signifies the importance of the distinction between what is private and what is public. Moreover, the term also connotes the sense of being alone or single; that is, there is a line drawn between what one is for himself or herself and the relation one has with others. Thus, the conception of the Romans and presumably other ancients was geared more toward the sense of "private" as in "private property." Roman law and custom was such that the master could do much more in his household than it is possible today. For example, he could sell off his slaves or children, or do anything he pleased with them with relative impunity. The reason was that he was the "master" within his private domain where the reach of the law was valid only for those who were free only, namely those who did not belong to any household or who were masters in their households themselves. Thus, there was a clear line between what is private and what is public, namely what is private belongs to an individual's property, lying within his disposal, where the public was where those individuals who had their private domains and properties interacted.[5]

This sense of "private" in the sense of "private property" and "private domain" still survives today with the legal recognition of the individuals' right to property. Furthermore, it also survives in discourse about the public/private distinction when it comes to attitudes toward women and domestic workers in the household, where the law does not seem to reach them as they do to people in public arenas.[6] However, the advent of modernity added another very important dimension to the sense. Instead of the private being understood to mean only the concrete private domain or property, the term became also understood to mean one's private "thoughts" and "ideas." This does not mean that the ancients did not have their private thoughts and ideas, but that the modern world became markedly different from the ancient one in that much more emphasis was paid to these private thoughts and ideas, in other words one's "subjectivities" which the moderns believed to be the underpinning of epistemology and hence metaphysics. As a primary and most influential example: according to Descartes, the foundation of all true knowledge

[5]Tamás (2002).

[6]G.M. Tamás, "From Subjectivity to Privacy and Back Again."

lies within an individual's sense of subjectivity of himself as a thinking, conscious being.

According to Tamás,[7] privacy was once the privilege of the propertied class, who enjoyed the "private" atmosphere of their homes. Vagabonds, refugees and slaves did not have any privacy because they did not own any property. However, as the conception became more subjectivized, the privacy of the individual came to mean increasingly that of the thoughts, desires and ideas of the individual herself. In one sense the thoughts and desires still belonged to the individual, in the same sense, generally speaking, as the land and other material properties belonged to the individual, but since the thoughts and ideas were not material and could not be quantified, the change was a significant one in that it underlined the metaphysical shift that took place as a result of modernity, namely the shift toward subjectivity in the Cartesian sense. What this has to do with our topic is that, the modern conception of privacy, being more subjectivized, points to more pronounced emphasis on information as what is being thought about and what can be collected in the mind of the subject. It is not enough just to defend privacy through a system of rights that recognize people's private, concrete properties, their thoughts, feelings, and sensibilities needed to be accounted for also.

This historical shift in the attitude toward privacy also points toward another important topic in the discussion on the general analysis of the concept. It is generally acknowledged that societies in the past did not pay as much attention to the protection of privacy as we do in contemporary times. In Thailand, for example, people lived in large households with little individual, private space; it was not uncommon at all for families to sleep together in one big bedroom and for children to be able sometimes to witness their parent's love making if the latter were not careful. There was also a closeness and a sense of trust among the family members and those who lived within close proximities toward one another. People shared their thoughts and feelings with one another seemingly more readily in this kind of social setting than in today's world.[8] Furthermore, since the system of government was not as sophisticated and technology-laden as it is today, there was little effort or possibility by the authorities to snoop upon people's private lives, unless it was a matter of 'spying' on people using techniques such as eavesdropping and so on. There was also a possibility of the practice of neighbors informing the authorities of their neighbor's suspicious activities. However, such activities did not, of course, achieve the same level of comprehensiveness and depth enjoyed by today's authorities who have a large variety of technological tools at their disposal to enter upon people's private lives. Hence, it seems fair to say that privacy as we know it today did not quite exist in past or in traditional societies.

However, this viewpoint is disputed in a number of research works dealing with anthropological investigations of the concept. According to Robert Murphy, privacy was universally recognized in all societies as a necessary tool whereby people

---

[7]G.M. Tamás, "From Subjectivity to Privacy and Back Again."

[8]See, for example, Ramasoota (2000). See also Ramasoota (1998).

earn trust toward one another, trust which is essential in establishing communication.[9] It is essential in establishing a sense of the self and in social relationships. Murphy also holds that privacy is necessary in maintaining relationships even among those who are close to one another, as a means of keeping certain distance in case there might be misunderstandings or ambiguities in the relationship.[10] However, one might need to compare Murphy's view here with the view proposed here in the book, which is more concerned with how the information pertaining to an individual might be used by the authorities or how one could protect the integrity of one's own sense of self. It might be true that all societies exhibit the traits outlined by Murphy. That is, it might well be true that all human relationships involve some kind of distancing to a certain degree, including even the most intimate relationships. However, there is a difference between "privacy" in the sense of social distance as in Murphy, and the same in the sense of maintaining some kind of control over the information about oneself so that the authorities do not have access to it without permission. It is certainly possible for there to be the first kind of privacy (i.e., social distancing) without the second kind (say, in a fully totalitarian society), but if this is the case, then we still need an analysis and justification of privacy that does justice to the second kind, as well as the possibility to criticize that kind of society. To say that privacy has always existed as Murphy suggests could be taken to imply that there is no need to defend and justify privacy, because it is there all along.

In another paper in the same volume, Westin argues that, as an empirical matter, privacy is also universal in all societies. Practices such as covering of the genitals, having sexual intercourse in a hidden place, are considered private and shows that privacy is practiced in all cultures. That is true, but still the account leaves open the question whether the privacy considered here is the same kind of thing as the concept we are interested in this book. Practices such as having private conversations among trusted friends who do not want to share the information to outside circles may well be universal, but perhaps what concerns most people regarding privacy in today's world is that their private lives are being threatened by the new technologies and by surveillance by the authorities. In traditional societies, there can well be cases where the authorities, such as the village elders, eavesdrop on some of the members of the village or employ an informer to keep them informed of the movement of these members. This shows that in these societies, privacy as freedom from intrusion or eavesdropping by the authorities can exist especially if the members feel that they are being threatened in some way. Nonetheless, this does not seem to be the kind of privacy that is discussed by Westin. Covering one's genitals or not having sex in public is not the same as having one's information stolen by the authorities. If this is the case, then to maintain that the meaning of

---

[9]Ferdinand Schoemann, "Privacy: Philosophical Dimensions of the Literature," in Ferdinand Schoemann, *Philosophical Dimensions of Privacy: An Anthology*, p. 9. See also Robert F. Murphy, "Social Distance and the Veil," op. cit., pp. 34–55.

[10]Robert F. Murphy, "Social Distance and the Veil," op. cit., pp. 34–55.

privacy also includes behaviors belonging to human's social nature, such as covering one's genitals, may mislead one from the more important point, which is how privacy in the sense of freedom from intrusion by the authorities should be protected and justified. Hence, while it may well be true that all societies do enjoy some degree of privacy in the sense of social practice, this does not mean, and should not be taken to imply, that privacy as freedom from intrusion is a thoroughly universal concept and practice. It is perfectly conceivable that a society might be able to. Even though a society does enjoy all kinds of social privacy in Westin's sense,[11] it is still conceivable that these social practices could continue unabated while there is no privacy in the sense of freedom from intrusion by those in power at all. If this scenario is conceivable, then we can conclude that the privacy discussed in Westin is not one and same as the privacy that is being threatened in today's globalized and technologized world.

Definitions of Privacy

It is natural for a complicated concept such as privacy has a large variety of definitions. The discussion above, where the differences in how privacy is understood is mentioned, adumbrates how complicated the concept really is. On the one hand, scholars such as Westin and Murphy believe that the same concept applies in the case of a primitive tribe which maintains some distance in their communication among their member, as it is in the case of privacy of, say, a group of individuals who have their genetic profiles stored and manipulated electronically in a population database. However, I have tried to point out that doing so might stretch the extension of the concept too far to do any useful work.

In this section, we will review a number of definitions of privacy in the literature. The definitions we got from the discussion above refer to the conceptual connection the concept has, according Murphy and Westin, to concepts such as social distancing, trust, and the need for maintaining a level of decency according to the norms of the community. However, if we agree that there is more to the modern conception of privacy which is effective in helping us fully understand the situation nowadays, this conception needs to be supplemented. In any case, the question is: What are we protecting when we claim that we need to be protecting our privacy against unwanted intrusions? It seems that we are protecting access to our own lives in terms of our information pertaining to our identity, or our inner sphere of life where we do not want outsiders to know them or to make them publicly available. According to Schoemann, the various proposals of definition of the term start first with the claim that privacy is a claim, an entitlement, or a right to determine what

[11] See, for example, account given in Kitiyadisai (2005).

information one should allow others to have access to.[12] However, Schoemann is right in arguing that this definition begs the question of what is morally significant with privacy. If privacy as the right to control information intimately related to oneself needs to be protected, then there is something morally significant about it, and it should be the task of the theory of privacy to spell this out.

In fact providing definitions of privacy appears to be a thriving academic industry. In a well-known article, Fried writes: "It is my thesis that privacy is not just one possible means among others to insure some other value, but that it is necessarily related to ends and relations of the most fundamental sort: respect, love, friendship and trust. Privacy is not merely a good technique for furthering these fundamental relations; rather without privacy they are simply inconceivable."[13] In roughly the same vein, Parent states: "Privacy is the condition of not having undocumented personal knowledge about one possessed by others. A person's privacy is diminished exactly to the degree that others possess this kind of knowledge about him,"[14] where personal information "consists of facts which most persons in a given society choose not to reveal about themselves (except to close friends, family, ...) or of facts about which a particular individual is acutely sensitive and which he therefore does not choose to reveal about himself, even though most people don't care if these same facts are widely known about themselves."[15]

Furthermore, some claim that privacy means having control of access by others to one's information about oneself. Schoemann again objects that this definition begs counterexamples in a situation where one has lost all control one has over one's own private information, but still one does not seem to have privacy. A man who is naked and alone on a deserted island has lost control over who has access to the information about his body—were there someone else who is on the island, he or she will be able to see everything on the man's body, but we would think that he still has his privacy, since he is alone on the island. Schoemann's proposed definition, then, is "a state of limited access to a person." According to him, "[a] person has privacy to the extent that others have limited access of information about him, limited access to the intimacies of his life, and limited access to his thoughts or his body."[16]

Schoemann claims that an advantage of this definition is that one can then distinguish between having privacy and having the right to privacy. By claiming that privacy is a state of limited access to a person, one leaves open the issue of the legal entitlement to such a state, thus making it possible for there to be a distinction between the two. One can then suffer loss of privacy without having one's right to

---

[12]Ferdinand D. Schomann, "Privacy: Philosophical Dimensions," in *Philosophical Dimensions of Privacy: An Anthology*, p. 2.

[13]Fried (1968).

[14]Parent (1983).

[15]W.A. Parent, "Privacy, Morality and the Law," p. 270.

[16]Ferdinand D. Schoemann, "Privacy: Philosophical Dimensions," in *Philosophical Dimensions of Privacy: An Anthology*, p. 3.

privacy violated, such as when one willingly gives away information. Or in a reverse case, one can also have one's right to privacy violated without having one's actual privacy infringed, such as when the authorities routinely monitor telephone conversations of the citizens, but have not actually checked on a particular person. Hence that person's privacy is not violated, even though his right is.

Schoemann's definition does leave open the question what is actually meant by the 'person' whose access is limited, and another one of how much the limit should be. He gives three accounts on the person, namely information about himself, intimacies of his life, and his thoughts and his body. But perhaps there could be a case where the person himself or his privacy is not exhausted by these three conditions, such as when information, not of himself directly, but of something relatable to him, is obtained without his permission. The information does not even have to be relatable to him directly, but if that information belongs to someone who has an intimate connection with him, then perhaps it is conceivable that *his* privacy would be infringed too. Furthermore, there is the issue of the extent to which the limit on access should be determined. This shows that privacy is a relative concept, as Helen Nissenbaum also points out.[17] It is possible that what counts as violation of privacy for one might not be so for another.

In a different vein, Graeme Laurie argues that privacy should be viewed as "a state of non-access from others."[18] What he has in mind is a definition that combines two major strands of privacy, viz. spatial and informational privacy. Spatial privacy is the state of non-access to a person's physical or psychological self, and informational privacy is the state where others do not have access to a set of information pertaining to a person.[19] Furthermore, Laurie elaborates this, saying "privacy should be taken to refer to a state in which an individual is apart from others, either in a bodily or psychological sense or by reference to the inaccessibility of certain intimate adjuncts to their individuality, such as personal information."[20]

It is in fact quite difficult how the concept of being apart from others could be a defining characteristic of being private. There is a sense in which, necessarily, an individual exists apart from all others, since we have different bodies, personalities, life histories, and so on. But that does not necessarily mean that we all have privacy as a matter of course. According to Laurie, the definition is designed to combine the two senses of spatial and informational privacy in such a way that a common conceptual thread between them is recognized. However, by stressing only the "apartness" of individuals, it seems that his conception is perhaps too vague to be able to do any effective work.

It is not surprising that a very complicated concept such as privacy did spawn a large number of definitions. As such privacy is not different from fundamental

---

[17]See, for example, Nissenbaum (2010).

[18]Laurie (2002).

[19]For an account for the informational nature of the person, see Floridi (2006, 2014).

[20]Graeme Laurie, *Genetic Privacy*, p. 6.

concepts such as 'time' or 'justice' where precise definitions are very difficult to pin down. Nonetheless, everyone knows what time is (being reminded, of course, of Augustine's dictum), and everyone instinctively knows when justice is missing in a certain scenario even though they might be hard put to come up with a specific account of it. I guess that perhaps privacy belongs to this class of concept. We all know what it is; more poignantly we instantly know when we do not have our privacy (except those who might not be aware of their privacy when it comes to their interaction with modern, sophisticated technology that mines their data, but this is a topic for later treatment in detail in the book), or when our privacy is being taken away. So instead of trying to come up with a precise definition, I would propose that we at this stage rely on our intuitive understanding of the term. Later on when we deal with accounts or theories of privacy, the issue of defining it might not be so important after all. (Here I agree with Lucas Introna, who argues in the same way.)[21] The assumption here is only that, in order to propose a systematic account or theory of privacy, one does not need a precise definition of the term. Only a rather vague and intuitive understanding should suffice. Nonetheless, Introna does give a number of intuitive accounts of privacy, which should provide a clearer view of what we are really talking about here in this book. According to Introna, privacy does exhibit the following properties:

(a) Privacy is a relational concept. It comes to the fore in a community. Where people interact, the issue of privacy emerges.
(b) Privacy is directed toward the personal domain. What is deemed personal is to some extent at least, culturally defined. In general one may state that personal or private aspects of my life are those aspects that do not, or tend not to, affect the significant interests of others.
(c) To claim privacy is to claim the right to limit access or control access to my personal or private domain.
(d) An effective way to control access to my personal realm is to control the distribution of textual images or verbal information about it.
(e) To claim privacy is to claim the right to a (personal) domain of immunity against the judgments of others.
(f) Privacy is a relative concept. It is a continuum. Total privacy may be as undesirable as total transparency. It is a matter of appropriateness for the situation at hand. It is unfortunately (or fortunately) a matter of judgment.[22]

The complexity and the difficulty of privacy has led some scholars to effectively renounce the task of providing a definition of the term all together. Recently, Daniel Solove has proposed a new attempt at defining privacy.[23] Inheriting the idea from Wittgenstein, Solove argues that any attempt to provide a unitary definition of

[21]Introna (2000).

[22]Lucas D. Introna, "Privacy and the Computer: Why We Need Privacy in the Information Society," p. 190.

[23]Solove (2008).

privacy has always been, and will always be, futile, since privacy is a very complicated concept which has been used in such a wide range of areas that it is not possible to provide a single definition for it. Nonetheless, Solove believes that one could still regard the various uses of privacy as falling under some kind of umbrella, as these various uses do resemble one another in one way or another. Wittgenstein has proposed the concept of 'family resemblance' to refer to the situation where instances of a certain concept vary so much that a single, clear cut definition of the term is not possible but still the concept and the term denoting it can be used in ordinary discourse since these instances resemble one another, much like members of a family resemble one another.[24] Thus, for Wittgenstein, it may be the case that two brothers resemble each other and one of the two may resemble their mother more than the other. The mother then resembles her father, but when the grandfather is compared with the brothers there might not so much resemblance, and so on. Hence there is a chain of resemblance, the sum of which is enough for one to gather, in ordinary discourse, that these members belong to the same clan. In the same manner, Solove argues that instances of the use of privacy, ranging from Internet privacy to wiretapping on the telephone to attempts to peep into somebody's bathroom, are all instances of one and the same concept, even though there cannot be a single, unitary definition of the term 'privacy.'

According to Solove,

> In contrast to attempts to develop a unified conception of privacy, I contend that privacy should be conceived in a more pluralistic way. "Privacy" is an umbrella term that refers to a wide and disparate group of related things. The use of such a broad term is helpful in some contexts, but quite unhelpful in others. Consider, for example, the term "animal." "Animal" refer to a large group of organisms—mammals, birds, reptiles, fish, and others—and within each of these groups are subgroups. For some purposes, using the term "animal" will suffice. … As with the term "animal," there are many times when the general term "privacy" will work well, but there are times when more specificity is required. Using the general term "privacy" can result in the conflation of different kinds of problems and can lead to understandings of the meaning of "privacy" that distract courts and policymakers from addressing the issues before them.
>
> Nevertheless, it is no accident that various things are referred to under the rubric of "privacy." They bear substantial similarities to each other. The analogies between different things can be useful and instructive. We should classify something as involving "privacy" when it bears resemblance to other things we classify in the same way. … Similarity, however, is not sameness, and we must also recognize where the many related things we call "privacy" diverge.[25]

Solove aims at arriving at a conception of privacy from the ground up, looking at how privacy issues play themselves out in real lives and how the term is used and understood, and build from that. This is a change from the usual philosophical

---

[24]See Wittgenstein (1953), especially §§66–68.

[25]Daniel J. Solove, *Understanding Privacy*, pp. 45–46.

method of arriving at a concept totally a priori and apply that onto local instances. Solove discusses many instances of privacy, namely the family, the body, sexual activity, the home, and communications.[26] Instead of starting from an a priori concept, Solove proposes to look at what the problems actually are and view violations of privacy as interferences of integrity of certain activities and propose that these disruptions form the basis on which an understanding of privacy is developed.[27]

In short, then, Solove would like us to give up any attempt to provide a single definition of privacy, exhorting us to rely instead on ordinary understandings of the term as it is used in daily life. I have quite a lot of sympathy with this approach. However, in relying on the everyday conception Solove has to assume that such a conception is already clearly understood, for otherwise it is hard to see how a theory of privacy is possible. In building up a conception of privacy from the ground up, looking at how the term is used and so on, there is always the problem of how these disparate instances could be tied up with one another to an extent that a theory is possible. According to Wittgenstein, no theory is possible since the actual relations among the instances of concepts are not there. The family resemblances among concept are but *pragmatic* ground on which language and concept use are possible at all. Perhaps this is what Solove intends to do with the concept of privacy. Still it begs the question of what to do when people's understandings of privacy do diverge in the beginning, as seems really to be the case when privacy concerns and issues have pervaded the world's cultures.

Privacy and Autonomy

Privacy and autonomy of the individual are closely related concepts. However, they do not necessarily relate to each other. This point is in contrast with what is believed by many scholars, for the standard account seems to be that privacy is a necessary condition for autonomy. Without privacy, it would be very difficult, so the argument goes, to maintain any kind of autonomy of the individual. However, in a close-knit society where everybody knows everybody in very intimate details and where everybody trusts everybody else, it seems possible that autonomy is in existence although privacy is not. However, it seems more difficult to imagine a reverse kind of society where individuals enjoy privacy but lack autonomy. For that to be the case, the individuals in question would have to be able to distance themselves from one another in certain ways so as to maintain a degree of privacy. But they might not be capable of thinking for themselves or independently by themselves. Conceptually this is possible, but it is very hard in practice to find such a society. In any case, societies where people enjoy autonomy but do not have

---

[26]Solove, *Understanding Privacy*, pp. 50–65.

[27]Solove, *Understanding Privacy*, p. 9.

much of privacy are quite common. In fact, most traditional societies are of this kind.

There are many arguments supporting the idea that privacy is necessary for autonomy. In one of the strongest support for the link between privacy and individual autonomy, Michael Eldred discusses Beate Rössler's work, *The Value of Privacy,* where she defends privacy in terms of something that emerges from individual autonomy.[28] According to Rössler, one has a normative claim to privacy when one's autonomy depends necessarily on the realization of privacy; in her words, "the true realization of freedom, that is a life led autonomously, is only possible in conditions where privacy is protected."[29] Furthermore, for Introna the issue has to do with being observed. It is likely, so he argues, that one is more likely to behave according to the wish of others rather than of one's own free will when one is observed.[30] It seems that when one is observed, one feels being pressured by a variety of factors in such a way that one's judgments would be clouded by them. Again this would be a moot point in a thoroughly transparent society where trust absolutely prevails. However, in a transparent society there is a qualm, felt by Introna, that individuals in such a society might behave out of the mindset that values conformity over their own individuality, and presumably that signifies an erosion of autonomy. Indeed, Introna argues that transparency and accountability are concepts that require privacy as a precondition. Without privacy, it would be impossible for accountability or transparency to have any valid meaning. For Introna, "privacy creates the clearing from which autonomy, trust, and accountability can emerge."[31] A machine cannot be accountable because it does not have autonomy. Trust is also not possible without autonomy either, and as Introna has argued, privacy is required for autonomy because trust and privacy are necessary for each other. So these concepts are intimately interconnected, with privacy as the linchpin of them all.

It may be useful here to inquire how and in exactly what sense privacy is related to such concepts as autonomy, trust or accountability. We have already seen that privacy is related to autonomy in the sense that the latter seem to presuppose the former. Without privacy, it is difficult to see how real and functioning autonomy can be present. However, we have also seen that this is not necessarily the case. In the atmosphere where there is complete trust of everybody to everybody, privacy does not really have to be there in order for autonomy to function. The reason is that when there is complete trust, there could even be a situation where everybody knows all the details about everybody else (this is of course not possible, at least for now, but we are talking here about a hypothetical situation), an individual in that

---

[28]Capurro et al. (2013). Rössler's work is Beate Rössler, *The Value of Privacy*, R.D.V. Glasgow, transl. (Cambridge: Polity Press 2005).

[29]Beate Rössler, *The Value of Privacy*, p. 72, quoted in Capurro, Eldred and Nagel, *Digital Whoness*, p. 68.

[30]Lucas D. Introna, "Privacy and the Computer: Why We Need Privacy in the Information Society," p. 194.

[31]Lucas D. Introna, "Privacy and the Computer," p. 195.

situation could well maintain her autonomy when she makes decisions and judgments out of her own belief and free will. The fact that her details (inner as well as outer) are known does not seem to prevent that. If this is so, then privacy and autonomy are concepts which are very closely related to that of trust. When there is truth, there does not even have to be privacy, or enforcing of privacy rules preventing someone from 'snooping' on others without their knowledge or consent. So it seems that the need for privacy protection arises from lack of trust. Since lack of trust is pervasive in almost all human societies, the need for privacy protection then becomes almost universal. Furthermore, if one is not accountable for what one does, then there would be no means to sanction anyone's behavior, including snooping and violating others' private personal space. So if there is no accountability, it is very likely that there is no privacy either. On the other hand, in the hypothetical scenario where there is complete trust and lack of privacy as mentioned earlier, the trust seems to ensure that everyone already is aware that he or she is accountable for what she is doing.

Of course such a hypothetical scenario where there is complete trust is a highly ideal one and is unlikely to be found in reality. But that should not deter us from pointing out that privacy and concepts such as autonomy, trust, and accountability are distinct and their logical connections spelled out. This will help us understand the concept of privacy as well as these other related concepts better.

Privacy and Contextual Integrity

The account of how privacy should be justified I offer in this book bears many resemblances with Helen Nissenbaum's view on the contextual integrity approach on privacy, where basically speaking norms regarding privacy protection should vary according to different contexts.[32] As information technology has become increasingly pervasive, many are concerned about its possible encroachment on privacy; however, the way privacy is threatened and how privacy plays a role in social life in general does vary, according to her, among different contexts. How privacy is approached, understood, protected, and analyzed is different, for example, in health care than in the home, and both are different from how privacy is understood and accepted in the social media. Instead of a 'one size fits all' approach where the user is confronted with a dialog box asking whether she agrees to disclose her personal information in exchange for her being able to participate in a website, Nissenbaum proposes a more nuanced approach where different domains and different settings play a constitutive role in deciding whether and how much privacy protection should play a role and in what form. According to her,

> The framework of contextual integrity identifies the roots of bewilderment, resistance, and sometimes resignation expressed by experts and non-experts alike. According to the

[32] Nissenbaum (2009). See also Nissenbaum (2011).

> framework, finely calibrated systems of social norms, or rules, govern the flow of personal information in distinct social contexts (e.g., education, health care, and politics). These norms, which I call context-relative informational norms, define and sustain essential activities and key relationships and interests, protect people and groups against harm, and balance the distribution of power. Responsive to historical, cultural, and even geographic contingencies, informational norms evolve over time in distinct patterns from society to society. Information technologies alarm us when they flout these informational norms—when, in the words of the framework, they violate contextual integrity.[33]

In her earlier article, Nissenbaum argues for a conception of privacy in public, where the advent of information technology has made possible the kind of surveillance that was not available before the technology was available, where the surveillance underscores the need for a conception of privacy even in a public place.[34] A familiar example illustrating this point is an office worker who relaxes in her office and takes off her shoes. While she is in a public space—the office where she works is shared by many others—her taking off the shoes and unwinding is part of her private moments and the norms governing privacy in this case would be violated if someone were to snoop up on her and see what she is doing. In this case, there are different contexts that clash with each other. On the one hand, there is the context of the putative private space surrounding her desk and her office, and on the other there is the public space of the office itself. In this case she is making herself at home, as if her office has become part of her home where she can unwind. In this case, then, the norm governing her home, or her private space at her office, is markedly different from that governing the public office. She may be wearing her office attire and her makeup, signifying that she is aware that she is in a public space and that people can look at her at any time. Nonetheless she also remains in a *private* space because the office is part of her domain and she is not interacting with any customer or any other member of the public. Respecting the office worker's privacy in this sense is tantamount to respecting the contextual integrity that, according to Nissenbaum, governs her privacy in this case.

In other words, for Nissenbaum privacy is justified when the norms governing how privacy should be regulated in a particular context are accepted socially as norms. Nissenbaum herself prefers to use the term "personal information flow" which she believes avoids the ambiguities and endless discussions if "privacy" is used instead.[35] Here, presumably, personal information flow within a particular context is justified when the flow can go on smoothly without being unduly interrupted. Thus Nissenbaum's point is to analyze when a norm is or is not violated; her main point is not as much on why a particular norm that is in use in a particular context is justified or is accepted as the governing norm. In contrast, that is exactly what I set out to do in this book. Nissenbaum searches for a "middle ground" between the lofty height of abstraction and the nitty gritty ground level disputes, and she argues that the social norms fit with this middle ground. In her

[33]Helen Nissenbaum, *Privacy in Context*, p. 3.

[34]Nissenbaum (1997).

[35]Helen Nissenbaum, *Privacy in Context*, p. 4.

words, “Between the ground and the heavens, according to the picture I am imagining, is the realm of the social, and it is in this realm that contextual integrity fits. This middle realm holds a key to explaining why people react to real-world disputes in the ways they do and why they frequently express their alarm in terms of the erosion of privacy.”[36] However, social norms are made up by people living in particular times and places, and it is clear that these norms are not the same everywhere. Part of my attempt here thus is different from Nissenbaum's in that I intend to go a level deeper; that is I intend to look at the metaphysical level of how normative guidelines regarding privacy in various contexts arise and how they are ultimately justified. Nissenbaum makes it clear that her view is based on the premises of contemporary liberal democracies, and these are my promises in the book as well. My contribution lies rather in explicating exactly how the premises of contemporary liberal democracies translate to the working norms regarding privacy which should work in different contexts because after all they are norms that govern *privacy* as a single concept.

Privacy and Justice

Privacy is not only related to autonomy of individuals, but on a wider, social scale privacy also has a lot to do with justice. In fact, the concern for privacy of individuals could be regarded as a concern for justice. When someone has an unfair advantage over others, such as when one has the power to obtain information about others' personal and private lives whereas others cannot do so in return, this would be a clear case of injustice. Furthermore, the issue becomes a standard one concerning the relation between the individuals and the state. In the case, where the state has no justifiable reason to obtain private and personal information of the citizens, this would not constitute justice, and the individuals have a fair claim against the state on this regard.

It is precisely at this point where there is a conflict between privacy and justice. It is entirely possible that effort to realize some kind of justice requires some intrusion of privacy. If this is the case, then one has to decide which value trumps over the other. On this, Arneson has the following to say:

> Suppose we say that justice requires equalizing people's opportunities for well-being. On this view, if one person is badly off now because she never had any opportunity to achieve a decent quality of life, there is a justice reason to compensate her for her misfortune, whereas if another person is equally badly off now because she squandered the rich opportunities that were available to her, there is no justice reason to compensate her and there may even be a case for transferring resources away from her so as to improve the opportunities of those whose initial options were bleak. But on this view upholding egalitarian justice requires agents of society to ferret out the information about individuals that will enable these classifications of people into different levels of responsibility for their current fate.

[36]Helen Nissenbaum, *Privacy in Context*, pp. 10–11.

> Moreover, agents of society must make complex and discriminating moral assessments of people's conduct of their lives. To some, theories of distributive justice with these implications amount to rationalizations for a Big Brother state.[37]

Simply put, the state, in order to ensure distributive justice for their citizens, might need to obtain information from the individuals so that it has the necessary ingredient in their decision making of how best to approach their policies. It might be necessary to obtain some kinds of information from the households pertaining to each individual there so that the state knows how to proceed. So in order for the state to make any concrete decisions and to implement any measures that addresses injustice of entitlements and goods, they might need to infringe on privacy. Here the key issue is the relation between the individual and the state, a very old topic in political philosophy. Privacy seems to be a very individual matter, and to protect it sometimes runs into conflict with attempts by the state to ensure distributive justice.

Arneson argues further, however, that the infringement on privacy does not have to be too harmful to the individuals since the benefits that will accrue outweigh the loss. He compares this to a medical procedure where the patient has to undergo some pain in order to be cured. Thus it is apparent that Arneson trumps justice over privacy. If there comes to a choice between the two, it seems that one should choose justice first.

However, it is not clear that privacy and justice have always to be incompatible values. The question whether distributive justice raises its own problems regarding encroachment of individual liberty aside, there does not seem to be any prevailing reason why privacy and justice have to be an either or situation. Arneson's dilemma apparently rests on the idea that, in order to enact laws and regulations that ensure certain kinds of distributive justice, certain information pertaining to the individuals is required, and this means encroachment on their privacy. However, in a situation where the individual and public interests are perfectly balanced, or where the two interests merge ideally into one (in the Hegelian sense), then there would be no conflict. In such a situation, individuals willingly give up their personal information, trusting that the authorities involved do the right things to ensure justice. It is true that there is no privacy, but there is no conflict. Private interests and those of the public are totally merged. Here the distinction between having privacy and having the *right* to privacy is relevant. Individuals in this ideal scenario do not have privacy (since they willingly give up the information), but it does not mean that they do not have the right to it.

Privacy and the Individual: The Metaphysics of Privacy

One of the most interesting topics in philosophical discussions on privacy is the conceptual relation between privacy and the individual. If anything, privacy seems to be a quintessentially individual concept. Perhaps the most salient aspect of

---

[37] Arneson (2000).

privacy as a topic in social philosophy is that it functions as something belonging to the individual such that the state is not justified in taking it away without compelling reasons. We have seen that from the Roman times onward, privacy specifies what belongs to the individual and seems to presuppose a clear line between the individual and what is outside of him or her. What is private is something that an individual enjoys, a space for the individual to wallow without being observed. Private domain or private property are those that the individual who is the lord of the domain or the owner of the property to enjoy and to dispose of it and she sees fit. What many are defending when they are defending privacy is a kind of boundary demarcating a space that functions, either actually or metaphorically, as the individual's own domain where outsides are not allowed and where the individual herself is empowered to defend it if someone wants to intrude into the space without her consent.[38]

Many arguments purporting to justify privacy rely on the conception of human dignity for support. Privacy is needed so that the dignity of individuals can be maintained. Schoemann has the following to say:

Defenders of the importance of privacy have generally followed two related strategies:

1. Arguments designed to show that respect for privacy is a key component in the more general regard for human dignity. The appeal here is to such conditions as moral integrity, individuality, consciousness of oneself as a being with moral character and worth, and consciousness of oneself as a being with a point of view, searching for meaning in life.
2. Arguments designed to show that respect for privacy is integral to our understanding of ourselves as social beings with varying kinds of relationships, each in its way important to a meaningful life.[39]

The first line of arguments argue that, since individuals have their own moral worth, qua human persons, and since privacy is necessary for the expression or the viability of those worths (which include such notions as human dignity, moral integrity, moral worth, and so on), privacy is thus needed and is justified. Here the underlying metaphysical issue seems to be that these moral worths do in fact rely on the conception of the individual as substantive, objective, and self-subsisting entity. For an individual to be autonomous, she has to be able to make judgments of her own, and for that to be possible she has to possess cognitive ability in such a way that she is able to understand language and to be conscious of her self. Thus Schoemann's condition that the individual be conscious of "oneself as a being with moral character and worth" shows that the individual needs to be able to be so conscious, and this ability is a necessary precondition for the individual to be

[38]See Debatin (2011) on how the U.S. discourse concerning privacy, which still dominates in much of the Western world, emerged out of Fourth Amendment protections of private spaces belonging to individual citizens.

[39]Ferdinand Schoemann, "Privacy: Philosophical Dimensions," p. 8.

autonomous. The moral worth and the dignity then follow from the autonomy. Hence it seems that these standard arguments for privacy ultimately rely on a notion of the individual as self-subsisting, substantive and objective entity.

What this actually means is that for an individual to be able to be autonomous and thus enjoys moral worth and dignity, the individual herself has to be self-subsisting; that is, she does not need other individuals for her very being. If it were to be the case that the individual here would be the only individual in the world, this fact would not have a bearing on the question whether she deserves moral worth or moral dignity, since her relations to other individuals appears to be irrelevant in this regard. This seems to be the presupposition of the standard arguments that purport to justify privacy through conceptions of autonomous individual, moral worth, or human dignity. These arguments seem to presuppose the metaphysical position that individuals are self-subsisting, namely they do not need to be related to other individuals, or other beings for that matter, for their status as an individual person. If the individual in question happens to be the only human person in the whole universe (supposing that there are no other cognitively advanced being, such as thinking robots or angels), then her moral worth or dignity would not suffer even a little. This is because the fact that she is now alone in the universe is not relevant to the question whether she possesses moral worth or dignity. The moral worth and dignity belong to her simply *qua* human person. Her relations to other individuals do not seem to have anything to do with this.

Thus privacy according to these lines of arguments is needed because it follows from the metaphysical assumption that individuals are self-subsisting in the sense outlined above. Hence, if privacy somehow happens to be unavailable, such as in a prison camp, then the individuals in that situation stand in a very serious threat of having their moral worth and their dignity taken away. However, if we consider the hypothetical situation described earlier, one where there is complete trust among all the individuals and one where privacy is not actually needed because everybody is completely open and trusting toward everybody else, then it seems at least that privacy does not have to be necessarily tied up with moral worth and dignity as the standard arguments seem to require. In such a situation, individuals do not have privacy, but that does not seem to imply that they do not have moral worth or dignity. However, this does not necessarily imply that privacy can be any less critical to democratic values. One might object that in a political environment where there is complete trust in the authorities as described in the text, the condition for a "conscientious objector" who needs some private space to deliberate on the possible inadequacies of the present regime, and, in case where the regime is a legal but an immoral one, could come up with a realization that the regime needs to be reformed. Without the private space, the objection goes, it would not be possible for the deliberation and the realization to take place. However, the objection is premised upon the existence of a legal but immoral regime, but if the regime is completely moral and just, then the basis for the objection does not arise in the first place. Furthermore, in a completely open and moral regime (and a very hypothetical and highly implausible one), everyone would be entitled to her own private space as there will be no restrictions on how one goes about deliberating and thinking on one's own. In this admittedly implausible scenario, privacy could be lacking but moral worth and dignity remains intact. In fact the situation in which they are completely open toward one another and are respectful toward one another seems to imply the opposite. Each one in this situation enjoys moral worth and dignity even though there is no privacy. In the prison camp situation the link between privacy and dignity is such that when there is no privacy there is then no dignity is perhaps due to the fact that there is an obvious imbalance of power. The prison guards, ordering the prisoners to strip naked and so on, are responsible for threatening the dignity of the prisoners because they have more power and use that power in an unscrupulous manner. But in the hypothetical and admittedly implausible situation described above, there is no abuse of power. And there is no immoral or unjust law to be abused either, since if the law were unjust then private space would certainly be needed as a breeding ground for the conscientious objector to think up their resistance plans. If we could suppose that there can be such a scenario where all laws are just and everybody trusts everybody else, then privacy would seem to be unnecessary. In this case everybody is open to everybody else, no one harboring any secrets, but the dignity of each one is maintained because of the prevailing trust. That is what is lacking in the prison camp situation.

If this can be the case, then privacy does not have to be always linked up with dignity and moral worth. The question then becomes whether such a hypothetical scenario is possible at all. But we will have to wait until later chapters in the book for a satisfactory answer to this question. What I am concerned with here is merely the conceptual possibility of the scenario. If this can be the case, then to justify privacy through conceptions such as human dignity or moral worth that ultimately rely on certain metaphysical conception of the individual is suspect.

Privacy and Private Language

Another point in philosophical analysis of privacy is the relation between privacy as a social norm and the "privacy" we have as individuals who have our own private thoughts such that no one else can have access to. This is a standard topic in epistemology, when the topic concerns the "privileged access" of the first person. Arguments aiming to justify privacy through reliance on certain conceptions of the individual, such as through the moral worth or dignity of individuals that we have seen, appear to presuppose that individuals do have the capability to have sole access to the domain within their thoughts, their "private" mental domain. The individuals, as subjects, have privileged access to their own mental states. They alone know their own mental states in such a way that nobody else can. An individual, for example, can feel her own pain through her own phenomenological experience as the one who does have the pain, the subject of the feeling of pain. No one else can feel exactly the same pain as she does. Even though neuroscientists might succeed in locating the part of her brain that is responsible for her feeling that is not the same as the subjective; the first-person feeling of the pain because that phenomenological quality is qualitatively different from the data presented on the brain scanner. As a consequence, her private thoughts and feelings appear to be absolute, and this underpins the notion that the individual deserves moral worth and dignity, since they are capable of entertaining such private feelings.[40]

The idea that the individual has sole privileged access to their mental states has much intuitive appeal. However, it has been criticized by a number of philosophers, most notably Ludwig Wittgenstein, who presents powerful arguments showing that the idea is incoherent. When one tries to make sense of one's private sensations, for example, when I tell myself, when I have certain sensation, that I am having an itch, I have to follow certain rules that make my meaning making activities systematic. That is, in telling myself and in somehow communicating to myself that I am having an itch, I have to follow the rule of English in the sense that I have to use the concept 'itch' which has its own systematic meaning. The meaning has to be systematic because if it were not, then the word would have no meaning at all, thus incapable of communicating any thought. Now Wittgenstein's point is that this systematicity cannot be arbitrary. This is so because, if meaning making were arbitrary, then there would be no systematicity and hence to meaning as we have just seen. But this implies that I cannot change how the words are used to mean anything by the sheer act of my will. I cannot, then, use the word 'itch' any way I like, and I have to follow the rules of English language even in making sense to *myself* that I am having an itch. Since I am constrained by this rule of systematicity, the meanings of the words I am using are not dependent on me, but in fact on the whole community of the users of English. For Wittgenstein this implies that the meanings of the words, even the words that refer to my own sensation such as my itch, are not private because if it were I would be able to change them arbitrarily. The fact that I cannot do so means that meanings are not private, and a rather startling consequence of this is that the content of my thoughts are not private at all, as it is possible in principle for another to learn about that content. In this case the meaning of 'itch' is the set of publicly available criteria that distinguish that kind of sensation from others, such as pain. The criteria have to be publicly available because that is precisely what the non-arbitrary condition requires.[41]

Perhaps there might be an equivocation here on how the word 'private' is used. Privacy as a social norm refers to a social condition where individuals are accorded respect by others and the authorities so that their lives are not made open for

[40]It is surprising that there is very little literature dealing with Wittgenstein's private language argument and information privacy. The standard work on Wittgenstein's private language argument remains Kripke (1982), where the argument is discussed in detail. A collection of articles on the topic is Jones (1971). However, after an extensive search I have failed to find a work that links up Wittgenstein's private language argument with a discussion on information privacy. Daniel Solove comes closest when he uses Wittgenstein's notion of family resemblances in his discussion of his pragmatic view of privacy in (2002).

[41]The *locus classicus* for Wittgenstein's argument against the coherence of a private language is his *Philosophical Investigations*, G.E.M. Anscombe, transl. (Oxford: Basic Blackwell, 1958), §244–271. For a concise and quick treatment of the complicated subject, see Candlish and Wrisley (2014).

everyone to see. On the other hand, in talking about 'private' language, Wittgenstein seems to be referring to some technical way of addressing language, in that 'private' language is the kind of language that only the subject has her own privileged access. (Such a language, it should be made clear here, does not mean a kind of language that functions like a code that the subject invents to herself which no one else understands because they do not know how to interpret it. Wittgenstein's argument against private language is much deeper. It says in effect that a language that consists of parts that only the subject can know because those parts refer to the subject's private sensation, or the first-person perspective of the subject herself, is untenable.) So it might appear that the two domains of use of 'private' or 'privacy' are distinct. However, when one considers that the main criterion of 'private' language in Wittgenstein's argument is that it is the kind of language that *only* the subject has access to, then the relation between this apparently technical use and the normal use of the term in social philosophy becomes quite clear. What is private, intuitively speaking, is something that only the owner has access to. This is true both for the more mundane sense of one's private plot of land or domain, or the sense of one's private thoughts and sensations.

In a recent book, Susan Greenfield argues that privacy is a distinctly modern phenomenon which did not obtain in the ancient world.[42] Her argument resonates with that of many others, such as Lawrence Friedman.[43] Friedman in particular has the following to say:

> In an important sense, privacy is a modern invention. Medieval people had no concept of privacy. They also had no actual privacy. Nobody was ever alone. No ordinary person had private space. Houses were tiny and crowded. Everyone was embedded in a face-to-face community. Privacy, as idea and reality, is the creation of a modern bourgeois society. Above all, it is a creation of the nineteenth century. In the twentieth century it became even more of a reality.[44]

Those who are familiar with the situation in Asia or other non-western regions should be very familiar with the picture painted here. One thing that emerges from Friedman's account here is that if privacy is a "modern invention," then it does not per se belong to the individual through her characteristic as a unique, autonomous, spontaneously rational being for the simple reason that these individuals were also present in ancient times when there was little or no privacy. Furthermore, Greenfield gave an account of the emergence of the modern novel, a literary genre that coincided with the rise of the middle class and the modern era. One main characteristic of the novel that distinguished it apart from the other, older genres such as the epic or dramatic poetry is that the novel relies on the first-person

---

[42]Susan Greenfield, *id: the quest for meaning in the 21st century* (Sceptre, 2008), pp. 123–124. Recently she has published another book, *Mind Change: How Digital Technologies Are Leaving Their Mark on Our Brains* (Random House, 2015), where she presents a scathing criticism of the use of information technology as a whole.

[43]Friedman (2007).

[44]Lawrence Friedman, *Guarding Life's Dark Secrets*, p. 258.

narrative of the characters. We are invited to peer inside the minds of the characters in the novel, and what is going on inside the minds of these characters does drive the plot of the novel forward. This was in a contrast with the older genre where outward action was the norm. According to Greenfield,

> Until relatively recently, up to the mid-eighteenth century, the social position into which you were born defined your identity, and broadly determined how you would live your life: there would have been little chance for a transformational inner perspective. … Not only would you have had much less time than nowadays for introspection, but the very notion of 'individuality' in our modern sense of being truly and complete unique may have been a lot less obvious.
>
> Then the Industrial Revolution came along to change everything. Just as a twenty-first century revolution in technology is currently transforming not only our lifestyles but how we might actually think and feel, so it must have been almost three centuries ago. … For the first time, Someone could be defined not just by their place and function in society, but by what happened to them in particular, and, most importantly, by the much wider repertoire of potential actions open to them.[45]

The main difference between the pre-modern and the modern individual is that the former was defined through his or her relations to others, whereas the latter is free to give his or her own definition of he or she should be. This is a key to the difference between the modern and the pre-modern conception of the individual and has a profound implication toward the conception of privacy. Viewed in this light, Wittgenstein's argument against private language is a critique of the modern conception of the individual which has as its basis the notion that the individual possesses the ability to link up mental episodes and their referent in a completely autonomous manner. This spontaneous autonomy then provides a basis for arguments based on human dignity. So the upshot is that if Wittgenstein is right in arguing that private language is incoherent, then all arguments for privacy based on individual dignity are incoherent.

It is, however, not quite a straightforward matter how private language in Wittgenstein's strong sense is related to the ideas of human dignity and autonomy that function as the lynchpin of the traditional conception or privacy. In order for Wittgenstein's private language argument to have an impact on the conception of privacy, a connection has to be established between it and the idea of human dignity and autonomy. In any case, one of the strongest justifications of human dignity and autonomy is that human beings are alone among all animals in being able to make meanings and understand them. In other words, humans are *rational* animals or perhaps more clearly language using animals. This has profound implications. In being able to use language, humans can construct models representing not only their immediate surroundings, but their future plans, their memories, constructions of the past, their desires for the future, and so on, even their fictional scenarios. Let us grant that this language using and understanding ability is what makes humans unique and thus is a basis for dignity and autonomy. It is a common idea that

---

[45]Susan Greenfield, *id: the quest for meaning*, pp. 121–122.

humans possess dignity in virtue of their ability to process meaningful symbols. However, the idea that humans are to be accorded dignity and autonomy goes further. Not only must humans possess language using and understanding ability, but it seems necessary also that there be a set of objective criteria whereby one individual human being can be distinguished from another. In arguing that human beings have dignity, the standard argument seems to start from the fact that humans are unique and another important step in the argument is that they are entitled to their individual, 'private' sphere. That is, they possess a 'world' which is theirs and theirs alone. Each individual human being possesses his or her own world, consisting in subjective experiences, thoughts, desires, episodes, memories and so on, which they do not share with any other. Chief among these subjective experiences are naturally those that refer to their sensations that they alone possess, such as their private feelings such as their itches and pains and so on. Now, then, we see the connection between the private language and the idea that humans naturally possess dignity and autonomy. So long as the idea of human dignity and autonomy is derived from the putative existence of subjective, first-person viewpoint constitutive of the private sphere, then there is a logical link between the two.

One of the most startling consequences of Wittgenstein's arguments against private language is that the putative private sphere of the individual alluded to above appears then to be destroyed. If there can be no private language, no possibility of referring to one's private sensations in such a way that only the subject is able to do, then it seems that there can be no individuals. However, that is rather far from the truth. From the statement that private language is an incoherent notion, one cannot deduce that no individual is possible. Individuals are possible, since they are obviously actual. There being no private language only means that there is no possibility of referring strictly to one's private sensations. The most one can do is to use publicly available language (or systematic language that can be learned—which is the character of all possible language) to refer to it. An upshot of this is that individuals still suffer from pains and itches, and they are still able to refer to them, talking about them and telling others about how they suffer and so on. But the meaning of their talks would then be public verifiable and sharable, not something that could belong strictly to one's individual domain alone.

Arguments purporting to justify privacy through conceptions of individual moral worth or human dignity presuppose that individuals are to be accorded these worths because of their ability to think for themselves or to be autonomous cognitive agent. It seems clear that the ability to think for themselves is closely related to the individual's ability to have their private sphere of thoughts and feelings. It is presumably in virtue of their having their private, individual spheres that individuals are autonomous, thus becoming candidates for moral worth and dignity. According to Deborah Johnson, for example, privacy is crucial because it is "an essential aspect of autonomy."[46] But if Wittgenstein's argument is correct, then these arguments cannot rely on individuals' having privileged access to their private

[46]Quoted in Moor (1997), from Johnson (1994).

spheres of thoughts and feelings as a foundation for the conclusion that privacy is justified. If privacy is to be justified as a desirable social norm, then the justification has to be of a different kind.

However, there might be an objection that autonomy can also be relational. That is, someone can be an autonomous agent, and one way of understanding Kant's system of ethics is that the moral reasoning that one entertains has a force on others also. In other words, the autonomous agent in Kant's ethics somehow needs the existence of others in order that her moral reasoning can carry force. For example, the categorical imperative says, briefly: Act in such a way that the maxim governing the act can become a universal law. Now the maxim can only become a universal law if the individual deliberating this is thinking of others, and is also deliberating on how one's action has a bearing on others. Without the others, then it looks like the categorical imperative does not have any force. However, the sense of 'autonomy' and an 'autonomous' agent in my discussion here is quite subtly different. It does not mean 'capable of standing alone' as much as 'not being subject to any higher authority.' In the sense of the objection outlined here, an individual, being capable of standing alone, might not be able to carry the force of the categorical imperative because the latter presupposes the existence of others so that the imperative can become universal. On the contrary, the sense I am rather using is the latter one of not being subject to any higher authority. It is part of not being subject to any higher authority that one must have one's own privacy, for intrusion of privacy is a clear sign that there is a higher authority capable of gathering information about oneself. Thus there is a clear line from autonomy, in the sense of not being subject to any higher authority, to privacy in this sense.[47]

In any case, justifying privacy will be the topic of the fourth chapter, where we build upon the material developed here and look at how to think deeply and justify privacy from the Buddhist perspective. Here we focus on the relations between privacy as a social concern and the private in Wittgenstein's private language argument. This relation is scarcely noticed in the literature, perhaps due to the fact that social philosophers do not pay much attention to the technicalities of Wittgenstein's arguments and vice versa. Nonetheless, one can see the connection between the two by noticing that one's private sphere of thought has become the foundation for the typical way of justifying privacy, as the former is the basis for one's autonomy and status as an autonomous agent. As we have seen, privacy is usually justified through the individual autonomy, and this autonomy seems nothing more or less than the individual's capability to exercise free thought. The 'free thought' here usually employs the kind of language that Wittgenstein finds to be deeply problematic, as we have seen. The reason is that such language presupposes the idea that one has a privileged access to one's own sensation in such a way that separates out one's own inner boundary from what is going on outside. This separating out then fits quite nicely with the drawing of a boundary between one's own private domain or private property and what is public as we have seen.

[47]I am grateful to an anonymous referee of the manuscript who points out this important out to me.

This does not mean, however, that Wittgenstein does not agree with the idea of free, autonomous thought, or that he thinks that thought should not be free. What the argument against private language implies is that usually the free, autonomous thought presupposed by most arguments purporting to justify privacy through human dignity and autonomy is in fact constituted by a number of different factors. One such factor is that the meaning of the words is objectively fixed by either reference to objective entities or objective criteria. For example, the meaning of the word 'itch' is fixed by the such-and-such feeling that one typically has when one is bitten by a mosquito. In other words there is a one-to-one correspondence between the sensation and the concept. It is this belief in such a correspondence that reinforces the belief that language is fixed in this way and that one's own private world of sensations such as itch and the like gives one a privileged access to knowledge, thus giving the world of sensation here a special place. This then becomes the basis for the justification of one's own private sphere as opposed to the publicly verifiable one that Wittgenstein prefers. It is as if language is a transparent medium through which one arrives at the meaning directly, where thought is realized at the level of the meaning or the proposition, and not on the level of public language itself. However, this transparency, as Wittgenstein argues, is possible only if private language is possible, for private language is just the kind of language that enables the subject to get at what the language means directly and transparently since the meaning is fixed by the subject alone. But we have already seen that this kind of language is incoherent. In the third chapter, this line of argument will be developed in greater detail, where Wittgenstein's attack on private language gives way to the Buddhist theory of privacy where the only way to justify privacy is through a pragmatic approach which does not presuppose that individuals need to be a self-subsisting entity as is the case in most liberal theories.

Conclusion

Privacy is a very multifaceted concept. We have seen that according to Daniel Solove, it cannot even be given a precise definition, since any attempts to do it would miss some important facet of the concept that is also recognizably an instance of privacy. Taking a cue from Wittgenstein, Solove argues that the concept could be understood more as a kind of 'family resemblance,' where instances of privacy are related one with another, but without an essential property linking them all together. Instead, such cases are linked through a chain of resemblances where one pair of the instances might resemble each other more than other pairs, but when an instance is paired up with a third instance, the new pair might resemble each other more than the others in their own way. This may well be the case, but still we would need to find a workable understanding of the whole concept, lest we fall into a trap where no definition or even no understanding of the whole concept can be found.

I have attempted to provide some definitions of the concept that are available in the literature. Perhaps more important than giving a precise definition is how to justify privacy. This will occupy the next chapters, but at least we have had a glimpse as to how this is to be done. No less interesting is the relations between privacy and other concepts, such as autonomy and justice. Here, one has to accept that privacy is a concept perhaps on a par with those of justice, freedom or autonomy in that they are basic to our understanding and our bearings in the world, so basic that it is extremely difficult to give a precise definition. Nonetheless, we can certainly discuss how privacy is related to these concepts. The fact that these concepts seem to be vague point to the fact that we are working at the fundamental level of philosophical, foundational concepts, and that any definitions we offer is very much a reflection of our own philosophical underpinnings.

Perhaps the most interesting topic that emerged from discussion of the philosophical ramifications of privacy is the relation between privacy and private language. The two are certainly closely related, as privacy is if anything a property that private language has. But it is surprising that there is little discussion of the relation in the literature. This may be due to the fact that privacy as commonly understood is a concept in social and political philosophy, whereas private language is more in the domain of logic, epistemology and philosophy of language. However, the two are certainly related, and I have shown that Wittgenstein's argument against the very coherence of the notion of private language demands equally strong argument to maintain or justify privacy as a social concept, which I intend to do in the chapter on the Buddhist conception of how privacy should be justified (Chap. 3). If there can be no private language, then it seems that there can be no privacy as a social convention or a social norm either. Or at least that is what I am trying to argue. We certainly have covered some ground but by doing so we realize that there is more than awaits much further investigation.

References

Arneson RJ (2000) Egalitarian justice versus the right to privacy? Soc Philos Policy 17(2):91

Candlish S, Wrisley G (2014) Private language. In: Zalta EN (ed) The Stanford encyclopedia of philosophy, (Fall 2014 edn). Available at http://plato.stanford.edu/archives/fall2014/entries/private-language/

Capurro R, Eldred M, Nagel D (2013) Digital whoness: identity, privacy and freedom in the cyberworld. Ontos Verlag, Frankfurt, pp 65–78

Debatin B (2011) Ethics, privacy, and self-restraint in social networking. In: Trepte S, Reinecke L (eds) Privacy Online. Springer, Berlin, pp 47–60

Floridi L (2006) Four challenges for a theory of informational privacy. Ethics Inf Technol 8:109–119

Floridi L (2014) The fourth revolution: how the infosphere is reshaping human reality. Oxford University Press, Oxford

Fried C (1968) Privacy. Yale Law J 77(3):475–493, 477

Friedman L (2007) Guarding life's dark secrets: legal and social controls over reputation, propriety, and privacy. Stanford University Press, Palo Alto, CA

Introna LD (2000) Privacy and the computer: why we need privacy in the information society. In Baird RM, Samsower R, Rosenbaum SE (eds) Cyberethics: social and moral issues in the computer age. Prometheus, New York, 188–199, 189

Johnson D (1994) Computer ethics, 2nd edn. Prentice Hall, Englewood Cliff, NJ, p 89

Jones OR (ed) (1971) The private language argument. Macmillan, London

Kitiyadisai K (2005) Privacy rights and protection: foreign values in modern thai context. Ethics Inf Technol 7:17–26

Kripke S (1982) Wittgenstein on rules and private language. Blackwell, Oxford

Laurie G (2002) Genetic privacy: a challenge to medico-legal norm. Cambridge University Press, Cambridge, p 6

Moor JH (1997) Toward a theory of privacy in the information age. In: Computers and Society, September 1997, pp 27–32, 28

Nissenbaum H (1997) Toward an approach for privacy in public: challenges of information technology. Ethics Behav 7(3):207–219

Nissenbaum H (2009) Privacy in context: technology, policy and the integrity of social life. Stanford University Press, Palo Alto, CA

Nissenbaum H (2010) Privacy in context: technology, policy, and the integrity of social Life. Stanford University Press, Palo Alto, CA

Nissenbaum H (2011) A contextual approach to privacy online. Daedalus J Am Acad Arts Sci 140 (4):32–48

Parent WA (1983) Privacy, morality and the law. Philos Public Aff 12(4):269–288 p. 269

Ramasoota P (1998) Information technology and bureaucratic surveillance: a case study of the population information network (PIN) in Thailand. Inf Technol Dev 8(1):51–64

Ramasoota P (2000) State surveillance, privacy and social control in Thailand (1350–1998), Unpublished Ph.D. Dissertation, Simon Fraser University

Scanlon T (1975) Thomson on privacy. Philos Public Aff 4(4):315–322

Schoemann F (1984) Philosophical dimensions of privacy: an anthology. Cambridge University Press, Cambridge, p 5

Solove D (2002) Conceptualizing privacy. Calif Law Rev 90(4):1087–1155

Solove DJ (2008) Understanding privacy. Harvard University Press, Cambridge, MA

Tamás GM (2002) From subjectivity to privacy and back again. Social Res 69(1):201–221

Thomson JJ (1975) The right to privacy. Philos Public Aff 4(4):95–314, 305–306

Wittgenstein L (1953) Philosophical investigations. Blackwell Publishing, Oxford

Chapter 3
Cultural Attitudes Toward Privacy

Introduction

As previously mentioned, privacy seems to be a distinctly modern phenomenon. The threats of modern technologies in surveillance, manipulation of large-scale data, and so on are only possible because of the technologies that are part and parcel of contemporary life. However, as these technologies spread to all corners of the globe, the problems arising from these uses do not limit themselves only to the West where most of these technologies originated. On the contrary, the problems find themselves also in new cultural contexts to which they are introduced. This gives rise to a new set of problems and issues, and in this chapter we will explore these issues in some detail.

Even though the issues of privacy, especially those arising from modern technologies, are clearly new, it by no means implies that privacy itself is a new phenomenon. Nonetheless, the context of the premodern society was very much different what our own today, and privacy, even though it might be valued, was in fact not available in many cases of the premodern or agricultural societies. Solove mentions that in colonial America most families share the same room together, and it was not uncommon for the husband and the wife to have sex discreetly with their children sleeping in the same bed (Solove 2008). In many societies in the past, the whole family shared only one room, as a result privacy was quite impossible. In urban areas, houses were packed together so much so that acts generally considered now to be private were not possible to be so, as things done in one house can be seen or heard by the neighbors.

One of the striking examples of how ancient people viewed privacy could be seen in the ruins of Roman latrines today. These are common latrines in the sense that there were no partitions between individual seats, so when people entered the latrine to go about their business they could see what others were doing in full view. This might sound shocking to us, but to the Romans this appeared to be a common occurrence, a general order of business of daily life. In many agricultural societies

S. Hongladarom, *A Buddhist Theory of Privacy*,
SpringerBriefs in Philosophy, DOI 10.1007/978-981-10-0317-2_3

in the East, relieving oneself is generally a matter of going to a rather secluded spot outdoors, such as behind a tree. Thus it was always possible that those doing this could be seen. This kind of practice can still be found even today. The distinction between the ancient and modern is also reflected in that between the developing and developed world that exists today.[1]

In this chapter, then, we will have a rather close look at how different cultures view privacy. However, what is perhaps more significant is a reflection on the conceptual or normative relation between privacy and culture. This will comprise the significant part of the chapter.

Privacy in Information Ethics: East and West

In the philosophical literature on privacy, much emphasis has been put on the definition of the concept and its justification. That is to be expected, because it is of course the task of philosophy to analyze concepts and to provide justification. In any case, what is interesting is that the majority of the works on the topic have been from the perspective of the West, and it is only recently that there is interest in what the East has to say on definition and justification of privacy. We have seen in the previous chapter that the volume of *Ethics and Information Technology* edited by Ess (2005a) is a pioneering attempt in filling this lacuna. In this chapter I shall lay the background for my own argument by first detailing what the major published works in the West have to say on privacy, and then we will have a look on some of the articles in the Ess volume. The discussion in this section will then lead to my own argument in the next section.

In "Toward a Theory of Privacy in the Information Age," Moor (2002) has perhaps a now classic conception of privacy. According to Moor, privacy consists in an expression of a core value that are held by all human groups; hence it is a universal value because being a part of the core values means that privacy is shared by all human groups. These core values are "life, happiness, freedom, knowledge, ability, resources, and security."[2] Thus for Moor privacy is a universal value and he disagrees with attempts to ground privacy as something that has only instrumental value.[3] Privacy in itself does not figure in the core values, but Moor claims that it is an expression of one of the core values, namely security. Privacy is an expression of the value of security because it protects us from unwanted intrusion that would rob us of the information that we hold dear to ourselves. For example, having

[1]In the US, the first census took place in the year 1790 in order to find out information about the number and make up of the US population so that the nation's capacity for industry and military capabilities. Census needs to be taken every 10 years in the US. See Measuring America: The Decennial Censuses from 1790 to 2000, available at http://www.census.gov/prod/2002pubs/pol02-ma.pdf.

[2]Jim Moor, "Toward a Theory of Privacy in the Information Age," p. 204.

[3]Jim Moor, "Toward a Theory of Privacy in the Information Age," pp. 202–205.

somebody wiretapping a person's phone conversations would be a blatant violation of her privacy, because it is regarded as phone conversation is a private matter and a society that does allow wiretapping to be widespread would not protect the security of its members at all. Moreover, the authority that does the wiretapping would violate the democratic ideal because protection of private information is crucial in ensuring the authority does not gain an unfair advantage over access of information which could well lead to abuse of power. For Moor, privacy is justified through its being an expression of the core values which all human groups and communities share. It is more an empirical concept than a normative one.

In addition, Moor calls for a "control/restrict access" conception of privacy where the individual has control over his or her own information through the principle of informed consent, and only those who are authorized to gain access to personal information can do so.[4] His example is a tax investigator who looks at tax records of certain individuals. So far as the investigator acts in his capacity as an investigator, he is authorized to do so, but only to the extent allowed by his work as investigator. As soon as he is snooping around and looks at the records just for curiosity, then he violates the principle, even though no new information is obtained.[5] For Moor privacy is more complicated than the simple "Either I know or nobody knows" scheme. The level of access that a person is allowed to gain access to another's information is defined through a complex of situations. Moor states: "Ideally, those who need to know do, those who don't, don't."[6]

Another conception is that of Moore (2003). He agrees with Jim Moor in that privacy is an empirically grounded concept and is universal in all human cultures. In support of this claim Moore cites a number of empirical studies in anthropology and cultural studies claiming that privacy is empirically grounded in all cultures, and thus is part of cultural universals.[7] He adds that though privacy is universal, its specific form does vary across cultures.[8] This topic of universality and empirical grounded of privacy will be the subject of the next sections. He differs from Moor in that he advocates the control-based definition of privacy, where privacy is "our ability to control patterns of association and disassociation with our fellows."[9] Moor would disagree with this, for he believes that it is not possible to control all the "greased" information about ourselves that is available through all the electronic means. Hence Moor's is a weaker conception that allows for some space in which personal information can be obtained, but only through authorized personnel.

In another well-known article, W.A. Parent defines privacy as "a condition of not having undocumented personal knowledge about one possessed by others" (Parent 1983). The idea is that if the personal knowledge in question is documented then

---

[4]Jim Moor, "Toward a Theory of Privacy in the Information Age," pp. 208–209.

[5]Jim Moor, "Toward a Theory of Privacy in the Information Age," p. 208.

[6]Jim Moor, "Toward a Theory of Privacy in the Information Age," p. 209.

[7]Adam D. Moore, "Privacy: Its Meaning and Value," p. 222.

[8]Adam D. Moore, "Privacy: Its Meaning and Value," p. 223.

[9]Adam D. Moore, "Privacy: Its Meaning and Value," p. 215.

presumably it is in a public domain in the sense that anybody can look it up and learn about the information without thereby violating the privacy of the person whom the information is about. Parent disagrees with those, such as Fried (1970) and Wasserstom (1979), who argue more toward a "control" conception of privacy where privacy is defined more as the control an individual has over the information related to himself or herself. According to Parent, an individual should be entitled to reveal as much or as little information concerning herself to those she trust as she likes. She has control over the information about herself, but it does not seem that her privacy is then either threatened or protected, because she voluntarily reveals her private information to others. She has control, but not necessarily privacy. Another important point in Parent's view is his justification of privacy. The reasons why privacy should be valued are threefold, according to Parent. First, if others have information of us they have power over us. Second, people are generally intolerant of others' lifestyles and so on, so privacy protects this, and lastly privacy is among the values that altogether constitute the "liberal ethics." In Parent's words, "individuals are not to be treated as mere property of the state but instead are to be respected as autonomous, independent beings with unique aims to fulfill."[10]

Hence it seems that Parent subscribes to the "instrumental" view of privacy as a value, since he believes that privacy is valuable because it brings about desired values, such as individual autonomy and protection against abuse of power by others, protection of diversity in lifestyles and so on, and the need for individuals to be treated as ends, not mere means, as Kant would say. This instrumental view accords with that of Fried, who argues for privacy as a necessary ingredient of intimacy among persons.[11] Their views thus contrast with those of Moor and Moore, both of whom look at privacy as a more or less universal concept. We will discuss this point later on when we look at how the Buddhists look at the problem of privacy later on in the paper.

What is common in these conceptions of privacy, even though there are many differences among them, is their presupposition of the existence of the individual or the self whose privacy is the object of analysis here. For people such as Moor, Moore, Fried or Parent privacy is that of the individual. The question is what it means for an individual to have privacy as well as why privacy is valuable or important to him or her. I would like to call this the "individual-centered" view of privacy because it seems to take for granted the existence of the individual self. Parent's definition, for example, presupposes that there be personal knowledge which should be protected from others. Moor's idea that information about oneself needs to be controlled and only restricted personnel are authorized to gain it in relevant contexts also shares the presupposition that it is information about oneself, that is, about the individual self who subjectively purviews the information about herself and decides which information could be divulged to others and which not.

---

[10]W.A. "Parent, Privacy, Morality and the Law," p. 276.

[11]See Charles Fried, *The Anatomy of Values*, p. 209.

This does not mean that privacy does not exist at the broader levels. According to Westin, there are three levels of privacy, that of political privacy, sociocultural privacy and individual privacy. The first is the kind of privacy that citizens in a political entity enjoys and can be violated only when the interests of the whole polity is at stake (Westin 2003). The second level concerns privacy in lifestyles, beliefs, behaviors, that should be protected from undue intrusion by the authority. In other words, cultures can also have their privacy as do individuals. The third level is that of the individual, whose private life should be accorded some space which would allow her to make decisions and express her ideas, which are necessary for democracy.[12] Thus Westin sees privacy to be a "social good," which requires "continuous support from the enlightened public."[13]

To turn to the right to privacy, Judith Jarvis Thomson famously argues that there is no such right (Thomson 1975); instead there are a group of rights related to the person which are more basic. Her argument is that the right that is usually considered as right to privacy is in fact right to some more basic conditions such as property or person. A quarreling couple, for example, might not enjoy their quarrels to be eavesdropped through a bugging device, but Thomson sees this more as the right not to be listened to, which is a part of the right over the person, not the right to privacy. Cutting someone's hair while she is asleep does not harm her, but her right is violated nonetheless, and that is the right over the person according to Thomson. The basic idea, then, is that any putative instances of violation of the right to privacy turn out to be, on closer analysis, to be violation of the right to person or the property.[14] Against this, Thomas Scanlon argues that there is indeed a common ground to the right of privacy, and that is the condition of "being able to be free from certain kinds of intrusions" (Sanlon 1975). And it is the intrusions of our bodies, behaviors and interactions with others are some of the clear examples of intrusions that violate the norm of privacy.[15]

From this brief review of the numerous literatures on privacy in the West, it should be clear that a common thread that runs though all these differing conceptions is the presupposition that the individual exists objectively and distinctly from other individuals. The control theory of privacy assumes that it is the individual that should be in control of her information. Nonetheless, there are views such as Nissenbaum's and Rachels' where the individual is considered as rather relational. According to Nissenbaum, what concerns us most about privacy is that it violates the norms expressed by what she calls "contextual integrity," where each area of social life (i.e., health care, the home, personal relations, information, etc.) has its own norms regarding privacy.[16] Furthermore, the relational and contextual account can also be found in James Rachels' discussion on the subject (Rachels 1975).

[12]Alan F. Westin, "Social and Political Dimensions of Privacy," p. 434.

[13]Alan F. Westin, "Social and Political Dimensions of Privacy," p. 434.

[14]Judith Jarvis Thomson, "The Right to Privacy," pp. 305–306.

[15]Thomas Scanlon, "Thomson on Privacy," p. 315.

[16]Helen Nissenbaum, Privacy in Context, *op. cit.*, p. 3.

The restricted-access view is also based on the belief that the individual exists access to whose information should be restricted. Parent views privacy as a protected given to personal knowledge, which is the kind of knowledge about an individual who, from her own first-person perspective, does not what others to share with her. The key issue here is the individual and the first-person perspective which is its defining characteristic.

This has not always been in the case even in the West. Tamás (2002) details the development of the conception of privacy in the West, and found that before the advent of modernity privacy consisted mostly in the "private" life in one's own house or among one's own family. It is only with the modern emphasis on the pure subjectivity of the individual (evidenced in René Descartes' famous "Cogito, ergo sum" statement) that the conception of privacy changed toward something based on the point of view of a single individual who is defined solely through her personal viewpoint, her idiosyncratic perspective which can be shared by no one.

In a critique of the modern conception of privacy, which clearly contrasts it with the ancient conception, Tamás has the following to say:

> Privacy as subjectivity hurts itself at the unchanging public sphere and at its political might, which makes the subject feels inessential, politically irrelevant; the subject still remains free to be herself, indeed the more herself she is within her private moral homestead, the freer she is; but in the public realm she is increasingly unprotected as long as rebellion is redefined as dissent and, of course, she has a "right" to dissent.[17]

So the ancient conception concerns having authority in one's homestead, and according to modernity such homestead has receded to lie solely within the limit of pure subjective consciousness, which as Tamás points out here, lies in danger of being eroded by the kind of politics which destroys the "public sphere" in which citizens exercise their right to take part in governance. What is interesting in our case is that all the key figures in contemporary debates and analyses on privacy in the West seem to subscribe to this modernist idea of "privacy as subjectivity." It is thus highly interesting to see how works on privacy from the Asian perspective compare with this Western conception.

As previously mentioned, Charles Ess has made an important contribution to this comparative perspective on privacy in his special issue of *Ethics and Information Technology*. The papers in the volume point to an emergence of a new perspective on privacy which does not rely solely on the metaphysics of "pure subjectivity" that we have seen to be presupposed by the Western conception. For Ess the most salient different between the Asian and Western conception is this basing of privacy on the individual subject, and he points out that this runs counter to the teaching of Buddhism:

> In particular, in those countries such as Japan and Thailand where Buddhism plays a central role in shaping cultural values and identity, the Buddhist emphasis on "no-self" (*Musi* in Japanese) directly undermines Western emphases on the autonomous individual as the most important reality (at least since Descartes), the source of morality (in Kant), the foundation of

[17]G. M. Tamás, "From Subjectivity to Privacy and Back Again," p. 220.

> democratic polity, and in all these ways the anchor of Western emphases on individual privacy. As Buddhism stresses instead the importance of overcoming the ego as the primary illusion at the root of our discontent – it thus provides a philosophical and religious justification for doing away with "privacy" altogether, as in the example of Japanese Pure Land Buddhism (*Jodo-shinsyu*), which inspires some authors to move towards salvation by voluntarily betraying private, even shameful personal thoughts (Ess 2005b).

Moreover, when the awareness of the need for privacy enters the lifeworld of the cultures of the East, Ess sees that what happened is a kind of "hybridization" where the elements of the West (individualism, emphasis on pure subjectivity) and of the East (emphasis on community and dissolution of the individual self) are mixed up. It is a purpose of this present paper to elucidate the nature of this mixture, and it shall be seen in the next section how a theory of privacy according to the Buddhist perspective could be started.

For more specific perspectives of privacy in the East, Lü provides a detailed analysis of Chinese culture in terms of privacy.[18] What is notable is that Lü states that for the Chinese privacy is regarded as having an instrumental, rather than intrinsic value.[19] And this will also be an important topic in the discussion of the Buddhist view which I shall develop in the next section. Furthermore, Kitiyadisai presents a powerful critique of the Thai government's recent attempt to issue "smart ID cards" to all its citizens, cards which have strong potential to violate the right to privacy of all Thai citizens.[20] As the much more personal information can be contained in the microchip that is implanted in the smart card, the potential for abuse is much greater than before. And more alarming is perhaps the tremendous power over the citizens that the Thai government could have once all the cards are issued to each citizen. (By law, each Thai citizen above 15 years old is required to have a national identity card.) This power includes population profiling, criminal records, genetic categorization and so on. Kitiyadisai correctly points out that the lack of legal mechanism against such abuse remains a thorny issue, and it appears that the government is not much interested in sponsoring a law which would restrict their own power.[21] Hence this is one of the many issues which the Thai citizens need to be constantly aware of so that the democratic ideal of checking and balancing the political power can be realized. The issue of state control and surveillance in Thailand as well as its threat to privacy is also studied by Pirongrong Ramasoota in her Ph.D. dissertation (Ramasoota 2000).

Another perspective comes from Japan. Makoto Nakada and Takanori Tamura says that privacy as practiced nowadays in Japan has its roots in traditional Japanese

---

[18]Lü, Yao-Huai, "Privacy and Data Privacy Issues in Contemporary China."

[19]See Lü, Yao-Huai, "Privacy and Data Privacy Issues in Contemporary China," and Ess "Lost in Translation," especially p. 2 and note 3.

[20]Krisana Kitiyadisai, "Privacy Rights and Protection: Foreign Values in Modern Thai Context."

[21]Krisana Kitiyadisai, "Privacy Rights and Protection: Foreign Values in Modern Thai Context."

culture.[22] What is emphasized here is the contrast between the Western notion of the individual as somehow atomic, where one is more or less separated from another, and the Eastern notion of the individual as defined in terms of the relations the individual is having with other individuals and of roles he or she has within the society.[23] This is a standard Confucian teaching on the individual in society (For more detail, see Ames and Rosemont 1988). The idea is reinforced by the Buddhist teaching on "non-self"; hence it is highly interesting to see how according to Buddhism (and to a lesser extent Confucianism) the modern conception of privacy as discussed in Western literature (such as those by Moor, Parent, or Moore and so on) can be analyzed and justified. In a paper in the Ess volume, Rafael Capurro also compares the Japanese concept of "denial of the self" (*musi*) with its Western counterpart (Capurro 2005).

In any case, a broad picture emerges from this comparative review of the literature on privacy: On the one hand, the West tends to view privacy in terms of a property of an atomic individual. Being atomic seems to imply that the individual is accorded some degree of privacy. This can also be compared with the ancient conception where one's private domain is the estate which one possesses and no outside influences are not to intervene (within certain limits). Breach of privacy is tantamount to trespassing one's property. The difference is that for the modern conception the domain in question has receded to the individual consciousness or "pure subjectivity." This is not to say that the estate or the individual possession such as land and other property has no role to play. Obviously these have a large role to play in modern societies, but it points to the fact that in the modern consciousness, the justification of privacy ultimately relies on pure subjectivity or private reasoning. Here one is reminded of the ethical principles of Kant, in which the ultimate linchpin of ethical judgment is the individual reasoning mind itself. To be sure, the reasoning mind reasons toward the universality of norms, which presupposes others, but it is still the reasoning mind herself that does the reasoning.[24]

On the other hand, the situation in the East, at least as emerged from the above discussion, tends to be one where the line separate one individual from another is fuzzier. One might want to compare this situation with the general social condition in Asia where individuals tend to live together in large family groups, sharing many things together, and where the need for private space is not emphasized. One might also imagine a large family house, where the boundaries among individual members are close to nonexistent. As for the private subjectivity, there is not much emphasis on it in the philosophical traditions of the East. Buddhism treats it as parts of the five constituent elements (*skandhas*) of the self, consisting of bodily form (*rūpa*), feeling (*vedanā*), perception (*saṃjñā*), disposition (*saṃskāra*), and

[22]Makoto Nakada and Takanori Tamura, "Japanese Conceptions of Privacy: An Intercultural Perspective."

[23]Makoto Nakada and Takanori Tamura, "Japanese Conceptions of Privacy: An Intercultural Perspective" and Charles Ess, "Lost in Translation."

[24]For a discussion of Kant's view on privacy and private thoughts and protection of freedom of expression, see Capurro et al. (2013).

consciousness (*vijñāna*). (This topic will be elaborated further in the next chapter.) The private self is thus composed of four basic elements in the Buddhist thought, and the idea of personal subjectivity is that it consists of these more basic elements. Hence one can see from the beginning that in Buddhism the personal self is broken down into these elements and there is no assertion that such a self exists as a self-subsisting entity. In more mundane terms, this could be taken to mean that in the East the emphasis is on the interrelation of one self with others, as seen in the Japanese examples mentioned in Nakada and Tamura,[25] rather than on the atomic characteristic as in the West.

Nonetheless, one should not be persuaded to have an idea that things are entirely black and white. The West has its interrelatedness of individuals as well as emphasis on the role of communities, and the East also has its way of emphasizing the separatedness of individuals. For example, the communitarian tradition, based largely on the works and thoughts of Hegel, is a clear indication that the idea that individuals are interrelated is not lost in the West. And in the East, today's globalized world has dictated that the idea of privacy is to take root and find ways of concrete realization.[26] The task for the theorist is then to search for a system of justification of privacy which does respect to these diversities of cultural traditions, but at the same time is powerful enough to command rational assent of all involved. In order to start to do this, we discuss in the next section the Buddhist view on the self and its implication for privacy.

Different Cultural Attitudes

Thailand

Pirongrong Ramasoota has documented attitudes of the Thai people toward privacy. As with other societies, Thai society in the past did not give much significance to individual privacy, and in fact it was not quite possible for people to maintain a degree of individual privacy in the modern sense due to the fact that family members typically shared rooms together. Moreover, when Thais migrated to urban areas as a result of economic expansion and industrial development, many lived close together, which made it very difficult to have privacy. Furthermore, Thai state in the past took an active interest in maintaining control over its population in order to secure manpower, which was a scarce resource before the advent of modern development and technologies. Ordinary Thai citizens were tattooed on the wrist to signify their obligation to the Crown. This was also a way intrude upon the privacy of the citizens as the tattooed wrist could be seen by anyone, so the tattoo advertised

---

[25]Nakada and Tamura, "Japanese Conceptions of Privacy: An Intercultural Perspective."

[26]See Lü, Yao-Huai, "Privacy and Data Privacy Issues in Contemporary China" for an example. See also Charles Ess's discussion of Chinese examples in his *Digital Media Ethics*, 2nd Edition (Cambridge: Polity, 2014), pp. 66–68.

openly the status of the person. Certain information could be put on the tattoo, such as the branch of the government the person had to work for, or to which noble masters the person belonged or had an obligation to.

The practice of registering ordinary citizens in Thailand is still being practiced today in the form of housing registration and citizen identification. The purpose of the housing registration is to specify the exact location where a citizen lives, which house number, in which district, which province and so on. Thus the authority has information on the exact number of population in each subdistrict, district, province, thus they are enabled to know the number of the population in the country, as well as their profiles. Another purpose is that the authority would then be able to link up any individual citizen to their domicile in the country. In addition to the housing registration, each citizen also has to carry a citizen identification card, which contains the name, sex, date of birth and the citizen ID number. The latter is a relatively new invention in the population registration system which made it possible for the authority to use huge population databases to manipulate information about the citizens, enabling it to group the population according to preset criteria. According to Ramasoota, these systems are tools that the Thai government uses to maintain surveillance on the population and the use has affected power relations between the government and the people in Thailand (Ramasoota 1998). This shows that, for Ramasoota, the attitude toward privacy by the Thai authorities is such that it may be an interesting idea, but not one that is actively defended in the law (Rananand 2007). Kitiyadisai also agrees with Ramasoota in that the traditional conception of what could be understood as a kind of privacy is collectivistic rather than individual (Kitiyadisai 2005). They agree that the conception of privacy as property of individuals has no place in traditional Thai culture.

According to Kitiyadisai, the word for "privacy" does not really exist in Thai language. What this actually means is that a new word has to be coined in order to connote the meaning of "privacy" as understood in modern context. This is true of Asian languages, such as Chinese and Japanese, as well.[27] Thai traditional village life was such that the whole family shared a room in common, a feature, noted before by Solove in colonial America, that did not quite promote individual privacy. Furthermore, Kitiyadisai reports that in the context of Thai culture, living closely together resulted in much emphasis being given on conflict avoidance, especially avoidance of face-to-face conflicts. Such avoidance is being strictly observed in Thai culture, so much so that it is almost a taboo to have open conflicts.

Another aspect of privacy in Thai culture concerns private affairs and noninterference in other people's lives. According to Kitiyadisai, "Personal or private businesses or affairs should not be interfered with in Thai culture, e.g., quarrels within the family, the punishment of a child by his parents, and so forth. This notion is the legacy of the feudal heritage of Thai society where the master or lord of the household owned and commanded the lives and destinies of all his subordinates

[27]Lü (2005) and Nakada and Tamura (2005).

under his autocratic rule."[28] This means that the master of the house had a free rein in running his house with minimum interference from outside authorities. Basically he could do what he pleased to the members of his household, a situation that was rather similar to the Roman house, where the master reigned supreme.

Ramasoota outlines a history of the concern of Thai authorities for registering and maintaining control over their population.[29] Starting from tattooing the wrists of the ordinary citizens, the authorities have sought to profile, categorize and control information related to the citizens in various ways. Thus the use of these systems reflects certain attitudes of the bureaucratic authorities toward the population in Thailand, an attitude that reaches far back into the past. During the period from the 1950s to the 1970s, Thai citizens were required to carry identification cards, which were launched in response to the Cold War and dictatorial rule which wanted to identify Thai citizens as distinct from foreign immigrants. The citizen identification card, together with the housing registration mentioned earlier, became then household items for all Thai citizens, something they seldom had a critical eye on.[30]

The advent of information technology in the 1980s gave rise to its use in maintaining a stronger grip on registration of the citizens. In 1983, personal identification number (PIN) was introduced to Thai citizens for the first time. From then on all Thai citizens were assigned a unique, 13-digit number that would immediately identify each of them instantly through the national database. The system then gave rise to the smart ID cards, which were introduced in the early 2000s. The card, as discussed before, could hold much more than the PIN. All this reflects the desire of the political authorities to control their citizens through information.

Apart from the cultural attitudes toward privacy and state control by the Thai authorities, Buddhism also explains much of the behavior and the attitudes that comprise the culture as a whole. Nonetheless, the connection between Buddhism and privacy is a highly complex matter which the later chapters will discuss in detail. Here we focus only on how much of the Thai culture could be explained through Buddhism. Ramasoota says that Buddhism is "incongruent" with privacy since Buddhism,[31] according to her, focuses more on otherworldly domain where individuals are encouraged to abandon the material world. This contrasts with the demands of the modern liberal society that stresses the importance of individual rights and freedoms.[32] More specifically she says that the two differ in two broad ways. First, Buddhism is based on interrelatedness or interdependence, whereas privacy is based on individual, atomic components of society. This is undoubtedly

---

[28]Krisana Kitiyadisai, "Privacy Rights and Protection: Foreign Values in Modern Thai Context," p. 18.

[29]Pirongrong Ramasoota Rananand, "Information Privacy in a Surveillance State," pp. 125–128.

[30]Pirongrong Ramasoota Rananand, "Information Privacy in a Surveillance State," p. 126.

[31]Pirongrong Ramasoota Rananand, "Information Privacy in a Surveillance State," p. 124.

[32]Pirongrong Ramasoota Rananand, "Information Privacy in a Surveillance State," p. 125.

true, but as I shall say in detail in the later chapters, this difference or apparent incongruence between Buddhism and the usual conception of privacy does not imply that privacy could not be justified through a new look or a reinterpretation of the Buddhist thought. Second, Ramasoota argues that Buddhism pays scant attention to individual right and freedom, which is the lynchpin of privacy. Again this will be a subject matter for further discussion in the later chapters.

China

The situation in China is in general not too different from that in Thailand. Traditionally, an agrarian society like the Thai one, Chinese society was one of very close knit families and village communities sharing a lot in common in daily living, especially living space. Thus privacy in the modern sense was quite unheard of. According to Lü Yao-Huai, all these changed in the 1980s as China was fast opening its door to the West and became more receptive toward Western beliefs, practices and ideas (Yao-Huai 2005). However, there is a large-scale historical study on the Chinese concepts of privacy, edited by McDougall and Hansson (2002), where articles are contained that argue for the concept of privacy in some sense was extant since the very ancient period in China. However, the studies in the book focus more on the attitude toward privacy as seen in the historical texts, thus are rather limited on the gentry or the aristocrats only. For these people there existed two separate realms, that of the *private* (*si*) and the *public* (*gong*). The former was regarded as a residual category, i.e., what remained after the latter domain was already delineated. In this case the situation was not much different from the ancient Thai society or Greek or Roman ones for that matter. The master of the household had his "private" domain inside his house where basically he could do whatever he pleased; this domain was contrasted with the public domain of the market or the government arena where the king ruled. However, in China, after the Taiping rebellion in the 1890s the situation began to change as the emerging middle class, or the capitalist class in the modern sense, began to assert themselves, thereby dismantling the age-old distinction between the gentry and the peasants. The onrush of Western ideas that flooded into China also included that of modern privacy, understood as the need for erecting an imaginary or legal barrier that is presupposed by the idea of individual right and freedom.

On top of this backdrop, Lü argues that the influx of Western, liberal ideas also had a lasting impact on how the lives of ordinary Chinese people were lived. More significantly, Lü's article focuses on the contemporary scene after the 1980s, where as *Chinese Concepts of Privacy* focuses more on historical matter. Since the opening up of China and the ever tighter integration of the country into the globalized world of economy and commerce, Chinese culture has to find for itself a place for the modern concept of privacy, which is presupposed by many beliefs and practices that are part of the modern liberal ideas. According to Lü, not long before the 1980s, the word for "privacy" in Chinese language was *Yin-si*, which could be literally translated as "shameful secret."[33] This is the kind of thing that connotes the old melodrama of a man having a mistress and having to hide this from the eyes of the public, obviously not something that could be a literal rendition of the modern concept of privacy. Furthermore, according to Manuel Maisog, "the traditional Chinese perspective sometimes assigned negative connotations to privacy. A lot of this can be seen from the Chinese language itself. For example, the saying 'to walk private' (走私) means 'to smuggle.' And the four-character saying 'self private, self benefit' (自私自利) means 'selfish' or 'self-centered.'"[34] This clearly shows the attitude of a typical Chinese toward privacy issues; it would take some time for the new conception of modern privacy to catch on. Nonetheless, Lü says that today the concept Yin-si has expanded to include those things that a person would not like others to know, which do not have to be shameful nor a secret. Thus even though it seems that the same word is still being used, it is used in such a way that the meaning has expanded quite significantly. This indicates a change in the consciousness of the language users as to how privacy should be understood. Nonetheless, even though Lü sees such a tremendous change in how privacy is conceptualized and understood in the Chinese context, he still believes that the conception will retain its Chineseness, a unique cultural trait that perhaps makes it always different from its Western counterpart. This is to be expected given the fact that concepts and language are tools that people use in their daily lives, and since there are still very noticeable differences in Chinese and Western cultures, despite the fact of the tighter economic integration, the existing differences will still be reflected in how words such as "yin-si" or "privacy" is used in the respective cultural spheres.

Another important point in Lü's paper is that he argues that for the Chinese attitude toward privacy is such that it is an instrumental value rather than an intrinsic one. Thus justifying privacy is a matter of showing positive outcomes when privacy regulations are followed rather than showing that it is the people's right to have their privacy protected.[35] For Lü this reflects the cultural background of the Chinese people that take the benefits of the whole to be of paramount importance. Perhaps what Lü actually means is that by protecting the privacy of the individuals, a number of social goods ensue, which do benefit both the individuals themselves and their society. If privacy is good for the society (perhaps through better and smoother relations with the West and the outside world), then the value of privacy is thereby justified. This, by the way, is also the position taken in this book, but in the later chapters I will argue for this instrumental justification of privacy in detail.

Recently, Charles Ess has discussed attempts by China to install systems that safeguard the privacy of their citizens, where the emerging legal framework closely

---

[33]Lü Yao-Huai, "Privacy and Data Privacy Issues in Contemporary China," p. 8.

[34]Manuel E. Maisog, "Personal Information Protection in China," available at http://www.huntonfiles.com/files/webupload/PrivacyLaw_Personal_Information_Protection_in_China.pdf [retrieved July 8, 2015], p. 3.

[35]Lü Yao-Huai, "Privacy and Data Private Issues in Contemporary China," p. 13.

resembles that of the European Union.[36] In the more liberal Hong Kong, the framework has been introduced as a necessary means to ensure smooth operations of international commerce. Moreover, the court in Beijing has ruled that privacy right is part of the "reputation right" of its citizens. Quoting scholars such as Sui and Greenleaf, Ess reports that developments in China are going along the path of the international community where there is an explicit legal framework that respects privacy rights which appears to be modeled on that of the EU.[37] These developments in Hong Kong and China are also reflected elsewhere, not only in the more advanced Japan, but also in Thailand and other developing countries in Asia.

Japan

According to Makoto Nakada and Takanori Tamura, the Japanese mindset regarding the issues of what is inner or outer is characterized by two words, *Seken* and *Shakai*.[38] Thus their central claim in the paper is that there are many layers of the Japanese conceptions of privacy due to complex historical, religious and cultural reasons. In other words the Japanese people live in a plurality of worlds constituted by their traditional worldview as well as the world as it appears through the need to interact with modernity. What is *Seken* resolves around traditional and indigenous thinking and way of life, whereas *Shakai* refers to the beliefs and practices coming from outside of the Japanese cultural world, especially from the West. For Nakada and Tamura, the distinction here is very important in understanding how privacy is understood and conceptualized by the Japanese mind. Presumably, as an introduced foreign concept, privacy obviously belongs to the *Shakai* world. However, it remains to be seen, and could be speculated, that Japanese culture also does have some conception and practice that could be related to privacy, at least to the way the concept is instantiated in the ancient world, as we have seen in the case of the Greek and Roman societies as well as the Chinese or Thai ones. Nonetheless, Nakada argues that another Japanese word should be added to the two, thus making a triangle of concept. According to Nakada and Tamura, *Ikai* is the world of "the other(s)," i.e., the hidden or forgotten meanings or values in *Seken* or *Shakai* as normal aspects of the world; *Ikai* is the aspect of the world from which evils, disasters, crimes, and impurity—along with freedom and the sources of

---

[36]Charles Ess, *Digital Media Ethics*, 2nd Ed., pp. 66–68.

[37]See Charles Ess, *Ibid*. The references to Sui and Greenleaf are Graham Greenleaf, "Asia-Pacific Data Privacy: 2011, the Year of Revolution?," UNSW Law Research Paper No. 2011-29, available at http://papers.ssrn.com/sol3/papers.cfm?abstract_id=1914212 (retrieved October 1, 2015), and S. Sui, "The Law and Regulation on Privacy in China," paper presented at the Rising Pan European and International Awareness of Biometrics and Security Ethics (RISE) Conference, Beijing, October 20–21, 2011.

[38]Makoto Nakada and Takanori Tamura, "Japanese Conceptions of Privacy: An Intercultural Perspective.".

energy related to art and spiritual meanings—seem to emerge. The term *Ikai* is furthermore sometimes used synonymously with *Muen*, which for Nakada and Tamura is crucial in understanding the Japanese mind more deeply.

In order to illustrate the meanings of these Japanese concepts and how they are related to that of privacy, Nakada and Tamura relate a story about a homicide that happened in 2004 in a small town outside of Tokyo. An unemployed 28-year-old man killed both of his parents and his elder sister.[39] The incident was reported in a rather lurid detail by the respected *Asahi Shimbun*, the national newspaper of Japan. The story contained details about the family as well as the detailed map and photographs of the family's house; it also included a story about the relations within this family and interviews of neighbors. To a Western or European mind this report is quite disturbing as it seems to intrude upon the privacy of the family, a tragic incident made even more so by the details of the newspaper report. However, when the authors asked their students about the report, most of his students did not see anything wrong in the report, saying that it was useful for the readers to know the background information and the truth behind the crime. Nakada and Tamura explain the situation by referring to the three concepts mentioned earlier. For a typical Japanese, the *Seken* is the normal functioning of things. This could be compared with the Greek term *cosmos* when it means the order of things, the way things normally are. When the crime happens, the typical Japanese mind would see this as a disturbance of the order, an influence coming from outside that disrupts the way things should be. The term for this disruptive force is *Ikai*, which could be compared with Greek chaos. It seems that for the Japanese *Seken* and *Ikai* are in perpetual conflict, as does the conflict between *cosmos* and *chaos* in the Western mind. Hence in fact both *Seken* and *Ikai* belong to the same cultural world. *Ikai* has its place in the indigenous Japanese mindset as does *Seken*, in the same as the hero and the villain both function in the same story. Thus the story in the *Asahi Shimbun* is an illustration of this ancient fight between order and chaos, between *Seken* and *Ikai*, that must have been played over and over in the Japanese cultural world for millennia. However, when Japan entered the modern world, there is an added dimension, that of *Shakai*, which refers to modern life, mindset, which obviously includes science, technology, economic globalization and the like. For Nakada and Tamura, the *Shakai* world means that the attitude toward the news report of the murdered family should be such that the private information of the family should be kept private, and this is in fact the standard practice in the EU countries today. According to the *Shakai* world, the private life of the murdered family should not be given in too much detail, but in the traditional mindset of the Japanese, just giving the outward fact of the crime would make no sense because one would then be at a loss in understanding how such a severe disruption of social order could have happened, and to answer this requires the notions of *Seken* and *Ikai*, which imply that some intimate details about the family and the location of the crime scene should be given.

---

[39]Makoto Nakada, "Japanese Conceptions of Privacy," p. 28.

The different attitudes toward how the news report of the crime should be given in the mass media show how the Japanese and the Europeans are divergent in their views toward privacy. For the Europeans, details about the victim's private life as well as his or her house location should not be shown in the report because these are seen not to be relevant to the gist of the report itself, and more significant because that would compromise the privacy of the family members of the murdered victims. The Japanese, on the other hand, view this as a strong disruption of the ordered universe through some blind outside force, and without further information regarding the victims private life and his exact location one would not be able to piece together how such a disruption could have happened. This is a clear example of diverse cultural attitudes toward privacy, something that will be discussed more later in this chapter.

According to Nakada and Tamura, there are two axes that define the relation between the "outer" and "inner" or the "public" and "private" in Japanese culture. One is defined as a relation between the *Ohyake*, which means "big house," and *Watakusi*, which means "not Ohyake," having the connotations of selfishness or being partial.[40] This relation stems from the premodern Japanese society where *Ohyake* means the imperial court or a place where big policy decisions are made. It also connoted the idea of the collective and what is impartial. *Watakusi*, on the other hand, connoted the idea of selfish or partial interests. Hence we can understand the relation between the two concepts as one between the collective and the individual interests, something not much different from the same kind of relation in Chinese, or other Asian cultures for that matter. This relation, namely the awareness of the opposite poles between the collective and individual interests, is deeply ingrained in Japanese culture. It is hardly surprising that positive value was given more to the collective than the individual. The other relation, on the other hand, is one between the "public" and the "private" in the modern sense. Here the word "privacy" is translated into Japanese, using the Katakana script that is reserved for phonetic approximation of foreign terms, as *puraibashii*, a word, with a sense not unlike the new connotation of the Chinese counterpart, Yin-si, denoting a new world where individuals' private sphere needs to be protected in the context of modern technological society.[41] Perhaps what distinguishes between the two is that, in the case of the old relation, positive value was given more to the collective (or the "public"), whereas in the later relation between the public and the private in the modern sense, it appears that more emphasis is paid to privacy—what relates to the individual as opposed to the large society—than to the interests of the public. In short, in the modern relation, as a result of the influx of modern or Western worldview, the private lives of individuals are given more positive value since this is part and parcel of modern society. This added dimension coming from the influx of Western worldview is what is lacking in the old relation between the "large house" and the "selfish interest" of the old Japanese culture.

[40]Nakada and Tamura, "Japanese Conceptions of Privacy," p. 32.

[41]Nakada and Tamura, "Japanese Conceptions of Privacy," p. 33.

In another paper, Mizutani et al. (2004) argue that one should distinguish between the descriptive and the normative senses of privacy. The empirical fact that one does or does not have privacy (such as when one is being watched constantly) is in the domain of descriptive privacy, and the rightness or wrongness of such action belongs to the domain of normative privacy. One may have a level of descriptive privacy when one walks along a street as no one is not bothering her, but that does not imply that she is entitled to normative privacy because, being on a public street, many people can look at her. Mizutani and others argue that even though the descriptive senses of privacy may differ in Japan and the West, especially the US, there is a certain minimally shared ground in the domain of normative privacy. That is to say, even in such divergent cultures as the American and the Japanese, there is a level of agreement that privacy of individuals should be protected. On the contrary the two cultures differ significantly on the issue of how such protection should be justified. Here Mizutani and others is quite different from Nakada and Tamura in that the former seem to be more universalistic regarding the value of privacy. Presumably, Nakada and Tamura's example of the lurid newspaper report of the murder might be looked at by Mizutani and others with not as much approval. For Nakada and Tamura, the way the newspaper gives a large number of details of the victim's private life signifies the Japanese attitude toward privacy that stems from their tradition and culture. However, presumably for Mizutani and others, such news report might have broken a normative rule of privacy of individuals. For Mizutani and others, there are two levels of the conception of privacy when it comes to cultural differences, namely the minimal and the rich levels.[42] The minimal level is what is shared across cultures; here Mizutani and others follow Moor's definition of "privacy" as "restricted access" (Moor 1997). Privacy is here defined as a situation where access to certain information is restricted to an individual or a group. In this sense only certain individuals or groups are permitted to have access to the information. On the contrary, information is public when there is no such restriction. Then Mizutani and others go on to provide historical details showing that restriction of access to information was also present in Japanese culture, and by implication in all cultures.[43] Having given a definition of the minimal level, the rich level is then understood as the traditions, histories, worldviews of a certain culture and all together constitute both the descriptive attitude toward and the normative understanding of privacy in that culture.[44]

---

[42]Mizutani, Dorsey and Moor, "The Internet and Japanese Conception of Privacy," p. 124.

[43]Mizutani, Dorsey and Moor, "The Internet and Japanese Conception of Privacy," p. 122.

[44]In fact Mizutani's conception of the minimal and the rich levels of culture bears some resemblance to my conception, derived from Michael Walzer in *Thick and Thin: Moral Arguments at Home and Abroad* (Notre Dame), that the impact of information and communication technologies on cultures could be seen at two levels, namely the thick and the thin one (See Soraj Hongladarom, "Global Culture, Local Cultures and the Internet," in Ess and Sudweeks 2001). The thick corresponds to the rich level and the thin to the minimal level here.

Though Mizutani and others went at a rather great length to show that the Japanese concept of privacy is a viable one and stands on a par with the conception of the privacy commonly accepted in the West, Yohko Orito and Kiyoshi Murata argue instead that the typical Japanese has a difficult time understanding the concept of privacy as manifested in contemporary, globalized practice.[45] For Orito and Murata, Japanese protection of privacy is superficial, presumably because the protection does not emerge out of a thorough understanding or a cultural background steeped in the felt need to protect the privacy rights of individuals.[46] The protection, as evidenced in regulations and laws in this regard, has only been put there as a result of pressure from the globalized world. Thus for Orito and Murata the right to privacy is not a universal one; instead it is an offshoot of Western mindset and tradition that is somehow imposed on other cultures due to the influences of the global economy. They conclude: "[I]t is not possible to claim that the sense of a right to privacy is a universal value."[47] Thus we have a pair of clearly opposing viewpoints on the status of the right to privacy in Japanese culture. On the one hand, Mizutani and others believe that such a right can indeed be a universal one, and one can find a root for the right from within the indigenous source of Japanese culture. However, Orito and Murata argue that such a right is a foreign induced one and there is no such right within the traditional Japanese culture. For the traditional Japanese, the concept that most resembles that of modern "privacy" has the connotation of a secret that one does not want to share because of one's shameful attitude. Thus the traditional conception here bears a striking resemblance to the Chinese concept of "shameful secret," whose characters are used to refer to "privacy" in the modern sense, as we have seen Lü argues before. Thus this is a very important issue which does not limit itself to only Japanese culture. In fact the issue affects all cultures where there is a conflict between the conception of privacy that emerges as a result of interaction with the globalized economy and the indigenous cultural tradition. This issue will be the topic of our next section.

Africa: Privacy and Ubuntu

Most discussions of the differences between East and West tend to ignore that there is a vast continent lying just south of Europe and southwest of Asia. This is unfortunate because Africa represents a very large collection of humanity and their myriad cultures, as well as rich intellectual traditions that could illuminate and strengthen the discussions in many ways. Recently there are very few scholarly

---

[45]Yohko Orito and Kiyoshi Murata, "Privacy Protection in Japan: Cultural Influence on the Universal Value," available at http://www.kisc.meiji.ac.jp/~ethicj/Privacy%20protection%20in%20Japan.pdf (retrieved July 8, 2015).

[46]Orito and Murata, "Privacy Protection in Japan."

[47]Orito and Murata, "Privacy Protection in Japan.".

works on philosophy of information in the African context, and the lacuna need to be filled soon if we are going to have a truly global perspective on privacy and other topics. Nonetheless, among the scant literature, there are those by Rafael Capurro, who has done more than any other scholars, I believe, to rectify the issue. Capurro has published many works detailing what is known as "African information ethics." Privacy, naturally, is at the center of the concern here. According to Capurro and others who are in the field, information ethics is based on the central notion of *ubuntu* in African philosophy. Basically the word roughly means "I am because you are," referring to the idea that the very existence of a self is dependent with the existence of other selves that the former self is in relation with. Capurro devotes a whole section in his recent work, *Digital Whoness*, to discuss this topic.[48] Basically, the principle of ubuntu is seen to be in some conflict with the idea of individual privacy as understood in the West. This is because the principle states that individuals are always connected with one another and that the core value is more a communitarian one rather than an individualistic one.[49] When it is conceived according to the principle that one's identity is derived from the connection with others, it is natural that privacy takes a back seat because the connections one has with others would seem to imply that one is completely open toward others. Capurro also seems to notice that there is a tension between the ubuntu principle and how privacy is to be justified here too.

The *ubuntu* principle is similar to the Buddhist conception of interdependence of all things where the identity, not only of individual persons, but of all entities whatsoever, depend on its relation with other entities. Thus, I believe that the conception of how privacy can be justified in the context of Buddhist theory of the individual and the self would apply equally well to the principle of ubuntu too. The idea is that the ubuntu principle does not, per se, conflict with individual privacy. But since the principle also emphasizes caring and being compassionate to one another, privacy is also included in the principle because in being compassionate to another person, one has to respect his or her privacy too. The principle that "I am because you are" is thus compatible with the idea of individual privacy because, in affirming that I am because you are, the identities of the "I" and the "you" are presupposed, and this presupposition consists in recognizing the privacy of others. In other words, by affirming that I am because you are, one thereby affirms also the identity of both oneself and the others one is related to. The idea of being open to others thus has to be limited by respecting certain boundaries that define the identity of the other persons one is dealing with; otherwise the respect of others as individual persons would collapse, and that would be in conflict with the *ubuntu* principle.

---

[48]See Capurro (2013).

[49]Capurro, "Intercultural Aspects of Digitally Mediated Whoness," p. 231.

References

Ames R, Rosemont H (1988) The analects of confucius: a philosophical translation. Ballantine, New York
Capurro R (2005) Privacy: an intercultural perspective. Ethics Inf Technol 7:37–47
Capurro R (2013) Intercultural aspects of digitally mediated whoness, privacy and freedom. In: Capurro R, Eldred M, Nagel D (eds) Digital whoness: identity, privacy and freedom in the cyberworld. Ontos Verlag, Frankfurt, pp 211–234
Capurro R, Eldred M, Nagel D (2013) Digital Whoness: Identity, Privacy and Freedom in the Cyberworld. Ontos Verlag, Frankfurt, pp 59–65
Ess C (2005a) Lost in translation. Ethics Inf Technol 7(1)
Ess C (2005b) Lost in translation. Ethics Inf Technol 7(1):1–6 (p. 5)
Ess C, Sudweeks F (eds) (2001) Culture, technology, communication: towards an intercultural global village. State University of New York Press, Albany, pp 307–324
Fried C (1970) The anatomy of values. Harvard University Press, Cambridge, p 141
Kitiyadisai K (2005) Privacy rights and protection: foreign values in modern Thai context. Ethics Inf Technol 7:17–26 (p. 18)
McDougall BS, Hansson A (eds) (2002) Chinese concepts of privacy. Brill, Leiden
Mizutani M, Dorsey J, Moor JH (2004) The internet and Japanese Conception of Privacy. Ethics Inf Technol 6:121–128
Moor JH (1997) Towards a theory of privacy in the information age. Comput Soc 27(3):27–32
Moor J (2002) Toward a theory of privacy in the information age. In: Baird RM, Ramsower R, Rosenbaum SE (eds) Cyberethics: social & moral issues in the computer age. Prometheus Books, Amherst, pp 200–212
Moore AD (2003) Privacy: its meaning and value. Am Philos Q 40(3):215–227
Nakada M, Tamura T (2005) Japanese conceptions of privacy: an intercultural perspective. Ethics Inf Technol 7:27–36
Parent WA (1983) Privacy, morality and the law. Philos Public Aff 12(4):269–288
Rachels J (1975) Why privacy is important. Philos Public Aff 4(4):323–333
Ramasoota P (1998) Information technology and bureaucrative surveillance: a case study of the population information network (PIN) in Thailand. Inf Technol Dev 8(1):51–64
Ramasoota P (2000) State surveillance, privacy and social control in Thailand (1350–1998). Unpublished Ph.D. Dissertation, Simon Fraser University
Rananand PR (2007) Information privacy in a surveillance state: a perspective from Thailand. In: Hongladarom S, Ess C (eds) Information technology ethics: cultural perspectives. Idea Group Reference, Hershey, pp 124–137
Scanlon T (1975) Thomson on privacy. Philos Public Aff 4(4):315–322
Solove D (2008) Understanding privacy. Harvard University Press, Cambridge, p 55
Tamás GM (2002) From subjectivity to privacy and back again. Soc Res 69(1):201–221
Thomson JJ (1975) The right to privacy. Philos Public Aff 4(4):295–314
Wasserstom R (1979) Privacy: some assumptions and arguments. In: Bronaugh R (ed) Philosophical law. Greenwood Press, Greenwood, pp 148–167
Westin AF (2003) Social and political dimensions of privacy. J Soc Issues 59(2):431–453
Yao-Huai L (2005) Privacy and data privacy issues in contemporary China. Ethics Inf Technol 7:7–15

Chapter 4
A Buddhist Theory of Privacy

Introduction

This is the central chapter of the book. I intend to present how privacy is justified according to the Buddhist perspective. My central argument is that the Buddhist perspective gives rise to a way of justifying privacy which is *pragmatic*. We have seen in Chap. 1 how Wittgenstein's private language argument, where he argues very convincingly that the very notion of private language itself is incoherent, leaves the attempt to ground information privacy on the objective structure of meaning (which is a corollary to the objective status of the individual as an autonomous, self-subsisting being) rather devastated. The only way out, I contend, is through the pragmatic conception which I outline here based on Buddhist philosophy. And in order to do just that I will begin with a brief account of the individual and the self in Buddhism. This is an introduction to the well-known Doctrine of the Non-Self, which is unique to Buddhism and has generated the most controversies throughout the centuries. Then I present how the Doctrine of Non-Self could give rise or support the view of individual privacy that is the same as the one accepted in the West. The central question to be addressed is: How is it possible that the individual self is regarded to be, in a sense, nonexistent and yet the privacy of that particular self can be justified? This apparently paradoxical notion cries out to be explained, which I do in this section. Then in the next section I discuss the notion of group privacy. Not only is privacy the right of an individual person, but, I argue, groups or communities have their privacy too. This means that the group shares some kind of knowledge or information together, and to attempt to intrude in order to gain access to this knowledge or information held by the group would be tantamount to doing the same thing to an individual. If by doing the latter one violates the privacy of the individual in question, one does violate the privacy of the group by doing the former too. Furthermore, the Buddhist conception where

S. Hongladarom, *A Buddhist Theory of Privacy*,
SpringerBriefs in Philosophy, DOI 10.1007/978-981-10-0317-2_4

individuals are only constructed from disparate elements does a better job, I argue, than any competitive theory at conceptualizing group privacy and justifying the notion.

Buddhist Theory of the Self (or the Non-self)

Basically speaking, the central tenet of Buddhism is that the self as we know it, namely the one who is thinking the thoughts, feeling the feelings, and so on, does not, strictly speaking, exist. This is a startling notion. However, the phrase "strictly speaking" is very important here. Buddhist philosophy does not say simply that the self does not exist. That would certainly be absurd. However, in a strict sense (which I shall elaborate later on) the self as we understand it does not exist in a way most people tend to think. Let us start to unravel this important argument in Buddhist philosophy here. The self here is understood as whatever referred to by the first-person pronoun. Thus when I say that I am now typing on a keyboard, what is referred to by the "I" here is a mixture of my body (since it is my fingers that are doing the typing) and my mental states (as I am trying to convey the complex meaning behind Buddhist philosophy into more or less understandable prose). According to Buddhism, the self as understood here is regarded to be a result of five *skandhas*, which is Sanskrit for "aggregates" or "heaps." In other words the self is understood to be composed of five factors or elements and these five only. These are: *rūpa*, *vedanā, saṁjñā, saṅskāra,* and *vijñāna*. These Sanskrit terms are conventionally translated as "form," "feeling," "perception," "volition," and "consciousness," respectively. The idea is that the self is composed of all these five elements and there are no other elements. If a property can be ascribed to these five elements together, then that property is said to be ascribed of the self itself. These five *skandhas*, in other words, serve as what present themselves to the mind when the mind seeks out a self. Thus, when I examine my self, what I find is always one or more of these five *skandhas* and none other. The five can be grouped roughly as the body and the mind; the first *skandha* (*rūpa*) is the body itself, and the other four are parts of the mind. Thus the five elements can be more simply regarded as a collection of body and mental episodes, which altogether comprise the empirical aspect of the self, namely what we find when we introspect what we understand to be our self.

One of the most important texts where the Buddha talks about the Non-Self is in the "Discourse on Not-Self Characteristics" or *Anatta-Lakkhana Sutta* in Pāli. Let us look at the following excerpt from the Discourse:

> Thus it was heard by me. At one time the Blessed One was living in the deer park of Isipatana near Benares. There, indeed, the Blessed One addressed the group of five monks.
>
> "Form, O monks, is not-self; if form were self, then form would not lead to affliction and it should obtain regarding form: 'May my form be thus, may my form not be thus'; and indeed, O monks, since form is not-self, therefore form leads to affliction and it does not obtain regarding form: 'May my form be thus, may my form not be thus.'"

"Feeling, O monks, is not-self; if feeling were self, then feeling would not lead to affliction and it should obtain regarding feeling: 'May my feeling be thus, may my feeling not be thus'; and indeed, O monks, since feeling is not-self, therefore feeling leads to affliction and it does not obtain regarding feeling: 'May my feeling be thus, may my feeling not be thus.'"[1]

The idea is that when we introspect our mind and our body to see what is going on with our self, what we find is that none of the elements that comprise the self (the *skandhas*) do not act in such a way that we would expect of our self. Thus what we normally believe to be our self in fact does not exist as we think. The Buddha's strategy in the text above is to get us to look at each of the *skandha*. If there is anything that is our self, then we must be able to control it. That is a very basic understanding of what it is to be a self. If *this* is to be my self—if *this* is going to be me, then I must be able to control *it*. However, inspecting each of the five *skandhas*, it is found that none of them can be controlled by us. We normally think that we can control our body; after all, the very fact that my fingers can move as I will show them that the body is mine and thus there is a boundary between me and what is not me. However, the Buddha asks us to consider whether we can always control our body. The key passage is here: "Form, O monks, is not-self; if form were self, then form would not lead to affliction and it should obtain regarding form: 'May my form be thus, may my form not be thus.'"[2] "Form" here is the conventional translation of "body." The idea is if the body were to be the self, it must not "lead to affliction;" that is, the body should always stay the same or the way we want it to be. But that is not the case because the body gets old or gets diseased, which we do not want. And the same goes with the remaining four *skandhas*. They have their ways of being which are independent of our wishes. We may think that the body has its own way of getting old which cannot be controlled by us, but the mind is even harder to control, as anybody who tries to control one's own thoughts can attest. The upshot is that neither of the five components of the self show the necessary sign of being the real self, and since these five components exhaust all the possibilities of being a self, the conclusion is that the self is an illusion.

In another text from the Canon, Buddhist master Nāgasena is having a conversation with the Greek King Menander (called in the text "Milinda"), who according to the legend had followed Alexander the Great to India but decided to stay there as king. There voluminous conversation is the subject matter of one of the great works in Buddhist philosophy. In this excerpt the two are talking about the nature of the soul:

The king said: 'Is there, Nāgasena, such a thing as the soul?'

'What is this, O king, the soul?'

'The living principle within which sees forms through the eye, hears sounds through the ear, experiences tastes through the tongue, smells odours through the nose, feels touch

---

[1]"Anatta-lakkhana Sutta: The Discourse on the Not-self Characteristic" (SN 22.59), translated from the Pali by N.K.G. Mendis. *Access to Insight (Legacy Edition)*, 13 June 2010, http://www.accesstoinsight.org/tipitaka/sn/sn22/sn22.059.mend.html.

[2]"Anatta-lakkhana Sutta: The Discourse on the Not-self Characteristic," op. cit.

> through the body, and discerns things (conditions, 'dhammā") through the mind—just as we, sitting here in the palace, can look out of any window out of which we wish to look, the east window or the west, or the north or the south.'
>
> The Elder replied: 'I will tell you about the five doors, great king. Listen, and give heed attentively. If the living principle within sees forms through the eye in the manner that you mention, choosing its window as it likes, can it not then see forms not only through the eye, but also through each of the other five organs of sense? And in like manner can it not then as well hear sounds, and experience taste, and smell odours, and feel touch, and discern conditions through each of the other five organs of sense, besides the one you have in each case specified?'
>
> 'No, Sir.'
>
> 'Then these powers are not united one to another indiscriminately, the latter sense to the former organ, and so on. Now we, as we are seated here in the palace, with these windows all thrown open, and in full daylight, if we only stretch forth our heads, see all kinds of objects plainly. Can the living principle do the same when the doors of the eyes are thrown open? When the doors of the ear are thrown open, can it do so? Can it then not only hear sounds, but see sights, experience tastes, smell odours, feel touch, and discern conditions? And so with each of its windows?'
>
> 'No, Sir.'
>
> …
>
> 'Then, great king, these powers are not united one to another indiscriminately.'
>
> 'I am not capable of discussing with such a reasoner. Be pleased, Sir, to explain to me how the matter stands.'
>
> Then the Elder convinced Milinda the king with discourse drawn from the Abhidhamma, saying: 'It is by reason, O king, of the eye and of forms that sight arises, and those other conditions—contact, sensation, idea, thought, abstraction, sense of vitality, and attention—arise each simultaneously with its predecessor. And a similar succession of cause and effect arises when each of the other five organs of sense is brought into play. And so herein there is no such thing as soul.'[3]

The main idea in this argument is that if there is a soul, or a self, who functions as the thinker and perceiver, or the manager of our thoughts and perceptions, then it should be possible for the manager to perceive things through other channels than the ones through which it normally perceives. For example, one sees with the eyes, and it is not possible that one sees through other organs such as the ear or the nose. One *only* sees things with the eyes. This shows that the eyes and the forms that are seen have to work together for sight to occur, and the soul or the self has no role in this. The eyes and the form seen alone are sufficient for sight to occur, and there is no need for a "living principle" which accounts for the seeing, or is the one who sees. If there were a self or a soul, then it has to be the one who sees (and hears,

[3]Nagasena, *Questions of Milinda* Book II. Chap. 6, available at http://www.sacred-texts.com/bud/sbe35/sbe3506.htm#page_86, retrieved Feb 20 2006. This particular text has been analyzed before in Hongladarom (2007).

tastes, smells, and so on), or to put it in another way the seeing occurs in the soul. However, Nāgasena shows that seeing can only occur when there is an appropriate connection between the eye and the thing seen (under normal conditions such as there is enough light, and so on), so the soul is not needed. And the same goes for the other sense modalities. As for inner thoughts, the argument goes the same way. The belief to be dismantled is that there is a "living principle" which does the thinking. However, thinking is accomplished by the thought faculty (i.e., the bodily organ that does the thinking) and the object of thought. But again only the thought faculty and the object of thought alone are sufficient for thoughts to occur, and this leaves out the living principle or the soul. Here the soul is taken to be the same as the self. Another way of explicating Nāgasena's argument here is that, whatever function that the soul or the self is expected to perform (such as thinking, feeling, sensing, etc.) can be done by a combination of the five senses or the thought faculty (the brain) and the object of senses or thought. Thus the soul or the self is nowhere to be found.

In conclusion, then, the Buddha's argument is that if something were to be the self, it has to exhibit certain characteristics, such as being able to be controlled, but we have seen that all the components of the self cannot be controlled, thus they do not exhibit the characteristics of a self. Thus no bodily form and no mental characteristic are such that they can be a self. Note here that the conclusion is not that there does not exist a self, but that what we normally take to be the self does not exhibit any of the characteristics that we believe are necessary for there to be a self. This, in a nutshell, is the Doctrine of Non-Self in Buddhism.

Buddhism and the Pragmatic Conception

Another important point that needs to be discussed here is the relation between Buddhist philosophy and the pragmatic conception that I am advocating here in the book. In fact I tend to use the two terms interchangeably: the Buddhist conception points to a pragmatic conception, and the latter is based on insights obtained from Buddhism. This is the unique feature of the book that I believe does a better job at explicating privacy and solving the many conceptual problems. Basically, the idea is that instead of searching for the one and only truth behind the phenomena, the philosopher should look at a broader context and find out what kind of purpose the search for truth is aimed at, or what kind of values or goals the search for truth contributes to realizing. Certainly truth itself is a value and a goal, but in many contexts to focus exclusively on truth tends to obscure the other types of values and goals that are already held by the members of the society. This does not mean that truth is discounted as a value, and indeed in many contexts the search for truth trumps over all other values. But in the case where there are other more pressing values and goals perhaps truth can wait.

Buddhism has a moving story to support this point. In one of the Suttas, or the collected teachings of the Buddha, the Buddha talks about a man who is hit by an arrow. The immediate task, he contends, is not to inquire about the identity of the archer, or about the type of arrow that was used, the trajectory of the arrow, how the archer shot the arrow, what shape the arrowhead had, and so on. Instead the immediate task is to help the man by getting the arrow out of his body as soon as possible and to clean the wound so that his life can be saved.[4] The point of the story is that, when a person is afflicted by all kinds of sufferings, the immediate task is to get him out of these sufferings so that he can be "saved" from having to wander endlessly in *samsara*, or the endless cycle of life, death, and rebirth that afflicts everyone unless they achieve final liberation. It is of no consequence to ask about the ultimate nature of reality, or the nature of afflictions, or whether people have free will or questions of that kind, for those questions are similar to the questions about the archer and the arrow, where the immediate task is to pull the arrow out and save the man's life. In order to save a person from *samsara*, then, one should go straight to the heart of the matter and stop endless disputes and debates that is the subject matter of philosophical speculation.

The pragmatic nature of the Buddha's teaching here is clear. The value that trumps all other values in this case is that of saving the man's life. Debates and discussions about the truth behind all other aspects of the shooting, the archer, the arrow, the bow, and so on are beside the point. The Buddha has a soteriological goal in mind (i.e., that the goal is to bring sentient beings to final liberation from *samsara*), and that is how to achieve Nirvana, where one ceases to wander life and life in *samsara*. Instead of searching for the truth behind all the phenomena, the Buddha urges us to consider what is really worthwhile and he tries ceaselessly to show that the purpose in life is nothing other than to realize that our lives are afflicted by suffering and that there is a way out of it. However, in our more mundane pragmatic consideration, we do not need to be that stringent. Nonetheless, the pragmatic nature of our enterprise in justifying and theorizing about privacy is that, instead of searching for truth in all aspects pertaining to privacy and its justification, we focus our attention to the value that privacy has in society. Modern informational privacy has clearly an important role to play in contemporary society permeated by information and communication technologies. We do not need to inquire about the truth behind all aspects of the situation—such as whether the individual is indeed autonomous because he is a self-legislating subject, whether he has free will, or any other question of the same kind; instead we inquire how privacy should be protected in such and such circumstances, and why. This would be much in line with the spirit of Buddhism.

---

[4]The story is from the Cula Malunkya Sutta. See "Cula-Malunkyovada Sutta: The Shorter Instructions to Malunkya" (MN 63), translated from the Pali by Thanissaro Bhikkhu. Access to Insight (Legacy Edition), 30 November 2013, http://www.accesstoinsight.org/tipitaka/mn/mn.063.than.html.

Doctrine of Non-self and Privacy

Among the vast literature on justification of privacy, perhaps the ones arguing that privacy is justified because individuals do have a right to their autonomy are the most prevalent. And among the numerous definitions of privacy, a common thread that binds them together seems to be that privacy is something that is cherished by the individual in question, something that she does not want to be exposed to the public gaze, and something that is crucial for the functioning and realization of democratic values. That could be the fact that she does not want other people to peer into her house, or data about herself, her "personal" information.[5] What justifies this right to privacy is that, as an individual citizen, she is entitled to some form of protection against unwanted intrusion, which is considered to be a breach of her autonomy. In a hypothetical polity where the state has unlimited power to take any information concerning its citizens as much as they like, and to have a surveillance scheme, Big Brother style, that provides every detail of the lives of the individuals, in that case it would be correct to say that the individuals do not have any privacy. What is missing is that the individuals do not have a means to operate without the seeing eyes of Big Brother. They do not have a leeway, so to speak, within which they can function on their own without always being aware that their action is constantly being watched. So we might call what is missing here "personal space" where the individual would feel to be free to do their things as they please, so long, of course, that these do not infringe on the rights and liberties of others. Talking about the potential loss of privacy by employees due to increased use of surveillance technologies by the employers, Miriam Schulman quotes Michael J. Meyer as follows: "Employees are autonomous moral agents. Among other things, that means they have independent moral status defined by some set of rights, not the least of which is the right not to be used by others as a means to increase overall welfare or profits."[6] Meyer then continues: "As thinking actors, human beings are more than cogs in an organization–things to be pushed around so as to maximize profits. They are entitled to respect, which requires some attention to privacy. If a boss were to monitor every conversation or move, most of us would think of such an environment as more like a prison then a humane workplace."[7] The key phrase here is "autonomous moral agents," and in fact we could extrapolate Meyer's statement to include privacy for individuals in general. The linchpin of a standard justification for privacy is, then, that individuals are autonomous moral agents, which imply that they are entitled to some personal and private space where they feel comfortable and where they do not have to behave as if they are being watched all the time.

So the standard justification of privacy is that since individuals are autonomous moral agents, they are entitled to some degree of privacy. This argument hinges, of

[5]W.A. Parent, "Privacy, Morality and the Law".

[6]Schulman Baird (2000).

[7]Miriam Schulman, "Little Brother is Watching You," p. 157.

course, on a conceptual link between the two. How is it possible that someone's being an autonomous moral agent entitles her at least some degree of privacy? Presumably the answer is that, as an autonomous moral agent, one should be accorded some degree of personal space, since if not, then one would not get the respect that one deserves in virtue of one's being a human being. When we consider the hypothetical state where nobody has any privacy as mentioned above, the standard argument would have it that in such a scenario the individuals are not paid respect to, since the authority (or the employer) has the power to gather all kinds of information pertaining to them. This presupposes that gathering information and constantly monitoring and watching the individuals all the time are not instances of respect. Thus we can sum up the standard argument as follows. As individual humans are autonomous moral agents, which imply that they are capable of making decisions by themselves and that they deserve a degree of respect, their private lives should not be intruded because such intrusion would mean that the intruder does not respect the individuals in virtue of their humanity.

However, this argument depends on some other crucial factors. What if the individuals in question willingly give up their privacy and allow the authority to watch their every move? In fact we are already seeing something like this happening with people putting web cameras in their bedrooms and turn them on all the time for all the world to see. Would we say that those who do this do not have privacy? But is their right to privacy being violated? It seems clear that simply the fact that somebody's private life is being exposed for the whole world is not sufficient for her privacy right to be violated. In this case it seems that nobody is violating her right, since she willingly does all this by herself.[8] Another factor is that the authority who has the power to intrude on people's private lives must act in such a way that harms those people through their intrusion; otherwise the authority's action might not be considered as a violation of privacy. The idea is this: Let us go back to the hypothetical scenario mentioned earlier. Nobody has any privacy; the authority has the all seeing power to know every small detail of their people's lives; nothing is hidden. Nonetheless, if the authority happens to be a wholly benevolent one and will not use the information in any harmful way, and if, in addition, the people are aware that the authority is watching them, but they do not mind since they trust the authority completely, then would we also say that their

[8]There is a growing amount of literature, however, on whether full autonomy—where only the person has the authority to decide—is desirable in all cases. Catriona Mackenzie, for example, has argued for a conception of *relational* autonomy where one's autonomy might be best served through the relations one has with others (see, Mackenzie 2008). Mackenzie's basic concern is what kind of autonomy is best for the patient, or those who are less than fully capable of deciding for themselves. The topic of relational autonomy has spawned a number of works debating the issue (see also Westlund 2009; Veltman 2014; Veltman and Piper 2014). I do not discuss the very nature of autonomy—whether it is relational in this sense—directly in this book. My concern is rather how to justify autonomy regardless of how the concept itself should be conceptualized. However, the topic of relational autonomy is very interesting and will be the subject for further research. For a critique of relational autonomy in the context of information privacy, see Beate Rössler, *The Value of Privacy,* quoted in Capurro, Eldred and Nagel, Digital Whoness, pp. 69–70.

privacy rights are threatened? According to Meyer, privacy appears to be an inherent property of an autonomous agent, but these scenarios seem to complicate the picture. Privacy may still be an inherent property in the case where people willingly put up webcams in their bedrooms and even their bathrooms, and in the case where the people trust the all seeing authority completely, but even so their inherent property here is not expressed. Even if the property is there, it lies dormant, so to speak, since the people willingly forego it. However, if this is really the case, then what is the difference between someone's having the inherent characteristic of privacy but it lies dormant and someone's not having the right to privacy at all?

The difference, of course, lies in the fact that in the first case someone could decide at any time to enforce her privacy right, which happens when, for example, somebody shuts down her webcam, whereas in the second case that is not possible. But if this is so, then the justification of privacy is not simply a matter of someone's being an autonomous moral agent who deserves respect, his or her relation with those around her also play a crucial role. If she trusts the all seeing authority completely, or if she does not think her private life should be kept to herself alone and welcomes the world to see all of her, then the trusting and the willingness to let others enter one's private domain become important. These are all relational concepts; one trusts another person, and one willingly lets others enter one's private life. After all, protecting privacy means that one is protecting someone's private domain from encroachments by others. If one lives alone, like Robinson Crusoe, then there is no need to even start talking about privacy.[9]

Another point is that it seems that one can even remain an autonomous moral agent without one's having privacy. In the scenarios described above, the one who trusts the authority completely, who lives in an environment where the authority is fully trustworthy, and who willingly foregoes privacy can still be an autonomous moral agent, since all her decisions are made through her free will in her rational capacity. An autonomous moral agent that willingly puts up webcams around her house is still so. But if this is the case, then the standard justification of privacy is in need of qualification. Being an autonomous moral agent alone is not sufficient, one also needs to relate with others and live in a certain kind of environment (such as one where it is not possible to trust the authority completely), in order for the right to privacy to actually have a force. Nevertheless, an objection to this line of argument is that in these scenarios the individuals always have their privacy rights all along, but as we have seen there does not seem to be much of a difference between having the right to privacy and keeping it dormant (perhaps always so) and not having it at all. This, let me emphasize, is tenable only in a very special case where the authority can be trusted completely and where the individuals are willing

---

[9]In the same spirit, Priscilla Regan also argues for the concept of privacy being relational, adding that the concept would be more useful if considered as relational rather than singular. See Regan (1995). See also Nissenbaum (2009), Rachels (1975).

to let others view their lives, and this could be extended to include the individuals' information about themselves, their communication, and others.[10]

In any case, relying on such conception as dignity makes privacy a nonrelational concept whose justification relies on the property of an individual. Thus it would be possible according to this system of justification for there to be only one individual person in the whole universe and he or she does indeed possess privacy, simply in virtue of her being an individual person. However, that seems counterintuitive. If anything privacy seems to be a relational concept, one does have privacy when others behave in one way (such as not snooping or spying) toward the individual rather than others. Proponents of the nonrelational view might say that the lone individual does have all the privacy she wants, because she is actually alone. Being utterly alone, however, seems to defeat the necessary requirement for there to be privacy in the first place. Imagine living alone without any other individuals around. Then the individual is in a sense utterly "private" that she is alone. No one cares anything about her because there is no one around. But then the lone individual could well be in a position where she is not strictly speaking private either. For being private requires that others respect her privacy and not snooping around her. Since there is no one around then this necessary condition of privacy is not met. So privacy presupposes relations among individuals. Without other individuals, or in a condition where there is only one individual in the universe, then it could not be said whether there is privacy or not.[11]

If this argument is somewhat cogent, then justification of privacy needs to take another turn. The argument above is purported to show that any type of argument relying on categorical properties of individuals such as their dignity or moral worth is suspect. Thus if there is to be a cogent argument for justifying privacy, then the relational character of privacy needs to be taken into consideration. What I would like to propose is that privacy could be more effectively justified through a recognition of the goal that privacy is designed to realize. This sounds simple enough but strangely this way of justifying the concept has not been much recognized in the literature.

The goals that privacy serve and realize are actually quite varied, but in any case it usually includes the restriction of the power of the authorities to gain unfair access to the information pertaining to particular individuals. Thus our example in the introduction about the Thai government issuing "smart" ID card containing chips which hold a large amount of individual information is a very appropriate

---

[10]Priscilla Regan, *Legislating Privacy.*

[11]In "Is Information All We Need to Protect?," *The Monist* 91.1(2008): 151–169, David Meeler argues that privacy should be best understood as protecting our information from being known by others. Meeler discusses another conception of privacy, one by Judith DeCew, where she argues that privacy is a cluster concept consisting of the ability to express ourselves withour fear, control how others have access to us, and a limit on the spread of information about us (DeCew 1986, quoted in Meeler, p. 153). In any case, however, privacy always presupposes the existence of others. Thus logically if one were to be absolutely alone, then one has no privacy, or to put it better the concept of privacy did not apply to one.

one. Here the privacy of Thai citizens vis-à-vis the state is justified because ensuring privacy is a key toward realization of the democratic ideals. Arbitrary mining of personal data without clear reasons is an example of arbitrary use of power which is contradictory to the ideals. In other words, privacy is necessary because without it real democracy would not be possible. Hence if democracy is to be the most preferred and defensible form of government, then privacy does have a role to play.

One main objection against the relational or instrumental view of justification of privacy is that the value of privacy then depends on the value of the goal which privacy purports to bring about. If this is so, so the objection goes, then the value of privacy is not absolute. But it seems, according to the argument, that the value of privacy is absolute because it seems strongly to depend on the autonomy and the inherent dignity of individual human beings. We have seen, however, that the idea of individual possessing the unique domain, or one's own "private" domain of thought depends on the viability of there being private language, but as Wittgenstein has shown, the whole idea of a private language is suspect; consequently the idea of one's private domain which is independent and well demarcated against others is suspect too. The upshot is that any argument purporting to justify individual privacy through their ability of forming and living in their "private" domain of thought is suspect. If there can be no private language in the Wittgensteinian sense, then there does not seem to be the case that there is, ontologically speaking, the individual private sphere either.

We have seen earlier that Ferdinand Schoemann distinguishes between two types of arguments aiming at justifying privacy. The first kind relies on the conception of moral worth and dignity of the individual, and we have just seen how this type is problematic. The other type of argument is instrumental. Privacy is needed because it functions significantly in the individual's sense of well being and her ability to function in her community. In Shoemann's words, privacy is "integral to our understanding of ourselves as social beings." Since we are social beings, privacy then is needed because presumably privacy is constitutive of us human individuals as *social* beings.

This argument is better than the first one in that it recognizes the relational character of privacy. Nonetheless, it seems too broad. Since we humans are social beings any way, then Schoemann's argument would be tantamount to saying that privacy is integral to our constitution as unique individual human beings. But it does not seem that way. Privacy as we know it today is a thoroughly modern invention. It is fair to say that ancient people did not have the conception of privacy, either spatial or informational privacy, as we know it today. People in ancient times lived in closed, almost cramped, conditions and their private space was nonexistent. A clear example of this is the Roman latrines, which consisted of rows of toilets on top of a flowing aqueduct with absolutely no partition in between, and it is said that both men and women did share the same latrine together. Even the upper class did not have any privacy, as every minute in the lives of royals was never alone, but always attended to by a host of "attendants," servants, royal pages, and the like. The situation was similar both in the East and the West before the onset of the modern, industrial age. If this is the case, then the idea that somehow privacy is integral of human life is not quite right.

So any attempt to justify privacy as we know it needs to take into consideration the values of our *modern* way of living. Justification of privacy then is part of justification of modern life, and of modernity in general. Since modern life revolves around the ideals and institutions of modern democracy, as well as its legal institutions and systems, then privacy cannot be considered in separation from these. As there is always a tendency in modern society for the political authorities to employ techniques by which they gain advantage over the citizens for any reasons, then I think the best way one could justify privacy is to rely on the need for ordinary citizens to guard against the encroachment upon their lives by the political authorities. It is clear, then, that in the modern society, individual citizens need to be protected from their own political authorities because the very ideal and viability of the democratic system depends on it. Without guaranteeing a set of basic rights to the individuals, the democratic system with its systematic check and balance of power breaks down, as the political authorities would be given a free hand to exercise their arbitrary power through their snooping around the private lives of people with impunity. If that kind of scenario is not acceptable, then any situation where privacy is not respected, or where privacy is breached for no clear and acceptable reasons would be unacceptable too.[12]

So what does the Doctrine of Non-Self have anything to do with privacy? I would like to say there is a great deal. As we have seen from the previous chapters, privacy is usually justified through reference to the individual, and the metaphysical assumption is that the individual is there as an self-subsisting entity, a self-legislating subject who possesses autonomy and dignity. However, my argument is that the existence of such a self-legislating autonomous subject is only contingent on privacy. In other words, such a subject is not necessary and there can be other ways to justify privacy for individuals under a different metaphysical conception, such as the Buddhist one that I have just outlined above. In fact I argue that metaphysical conceptions of an individual are in fact not relevant to an attempt to justify privacy for a member of a society in practical context. This is the gist of the pragmatic consideration that I am proposing.

Any attempt to theorize about privacy must first of all be adequate. That is, the conception needs to be such that it provides protection of privacy rights for individual (or their group, as we shall see in the next section) as much as needed for the individual to function well in society. Hence if more than one theory is equally adequate then there is no reason to single out just one as the uniquely correct one. To do that it would be required that there be a standard of correctness which lies beyond practical reality of how to protect privacy of individuals in actual situation. However, unless we are interested in pursuing "pure philosophy" where the aim is not to engage in how best to justify and theorize about privacy in the pluralistic

[12]See Debatin (2011) for a discussion of the history of development of modern individual privacy rights in the West, especially in the US, which appears to go along the same line.

contexts which define our world today, but to engage in debating about the "truth of the matter," we should be contented with the former. This is not to say that to engage ourselves in the latter pursuit is not worthwhile, but only that it is not directly relevant to finding out how privacy should be grounded in real life, especially in the context where there are other considerations which put more emphasis on there being pluralistic account of how privacy is grounded.

To illustrate, the usual way privacy of an individual is justified that, since the individual deserves respect because she is autonomous and has dignity, she thus has privacy rights as an expression of that respect. Now suppose that the individual has the same privacy rights but she is considered in the Buddhist way as not being grounded on an inherently existing self, then the privacy right and other rights can still be accorded to her because these rights are necessary components of the kind of society that we find valuable, such as a democratic one. We have seen in previous chapters how democracy and privacy are closely related. The idea is that an individual cannot be a fully functioning member of a democratic society if her privacy rights are taken away. That would mean that her life, her body, and all things related to her would be totally exposed, resulting in she losing all the necessary characteristics of a full member of society. She would be no more than a slave who has no life of her own. This type of arguing for individual privacy does not depend on the metaphysical assumption in liberalism of the autonomous individual, but the end result is the same.

An objection to this might be that the argument I am offering depends on accepting democratic values to be worthy of defending. However, it is hard to imagine how privacy and democracy could exist apart from each other. It is certainly possible, but it is not the kind of thing that happens in our modern world. A liberal and democratic society is one where individuals are accorded rights and freedom and where rule of law predominates; it is thus very difficult to imagine that there is no protection of privacy in this kind of society, for that would contradict the basic notion of liberal democracy as individuals would get no respect if they did not have privacy. Furthermore, democratic values are actually worthy of defending, and many countries in Asia, Africa, and other continents around the globe are indeed expressing the democratic aspirations in no uncertain terms. It is beyond the scope of this short book to lay out in detail why democracy is justifiable, but the fact that people all over the world are clamoring for it should at least be taken as a given that democratic values are worthy and that statements saying that these values are worthy should be taken as a premise. If that is so, then justification of privacy can be done through referring to these liberal and democratic values. This would certainly be an alternative to a conception of adequate defense of privacy apart from the metaphysical conception of the autonomous individual. The requirement is of course that in a democratic society it is irrelevant that what kind of metaphysics of the individual one entertains. One could accept the standard Kantian account, or the Buddhist account, but those accounts are immaterial when the topic is the role of individuals in a democratic society, where the point is the relation among them and the sharing of power in an equitable manner, rather than the metaphysical constitution of each particular individual.

In this case, is there then anything special in the Buddhist account of the individual that could lead to a justification of privacy? In the ultimate sense, the Buddhist account, the Doctrine of Non-Self, would imply that it is possible for persons to open themselves up completely toward one another. Since there is strictly speaking no self, there is then no boundary that prevents one person from completely merging with another. In this case there would be no privacy between the two. Perhaps an advantage of the Buddhist account is that it makes it conceptually possible for this kind of future scenario to take place. However, the merging here is only ethically possible when the two persons completely trust each other, so much so that they are willing to share all aspects of their lives together when they are confident enough, of course, that others will not harm them after they have opened themselves up so completely. In other cases, it is always necessary for one person to build up a fence, so to speak, that prevents others from intruding upon her life, to protect her privacy. Thus, in the Buddhist account instead of privacy perhaps flowing conceptually from autonomy, we have instead privacy as something that has to be consciously constructed. This could be as strong as one wants it to be.

What I have discussed so far concerns the Buddhist theory of the Non-Self and its relation to a theory of privacy, but is there any direct mention of privacy in the Canon, anywhere in the Canon that specifically discusses the issue? In fact privacy, or private space where one can be free from distractions, is important for the practice. Monks who have listened to the Buddha's teaching usually find a quite space where they can be alone to meditate and be with themselves without being distracted by others. Being free from distractions is an important factor in effective meditation, which is a crucial step in the practice leading up eventually to achievement of Liberation. In the Buddha's times these private spaces are usually some secluded spots in the forest (the Buddha and his disciples spent most of their time in the forest, and they traveled to the city only when they begged for food or when they were invited by householders) and started meditating on their own. This seems to show at least a level of respect of privacy of the monks. Furthermore, there are also numerous mentions in the text about the Buddha "resting in his private corner" when it is expected that nobody should disturb him during this time. In the *Mahali Sutta*, for example, visitors who came to talk with the Buddha were told by his students to wait outside of his private chamber for some hours when the Buddha was resting inside. Here the Thai translation says that the Buddha "resides in his private chamber," but the English translation puts it that the Buddha "is in solitary meditation."[13] In any case, he is not available to meet his visitors until he comes out of his private room, or out of his meditation, whichever the case may be. And the two translations point to the fact that the Buddha's privacy was respected, which shows that there is a recognition of the importance of privacy in the early Buddhist texts. However, as for the theory and justification privacy in the information age,

[13]See, for example Sutta (1995).

we have to wait until today to talk about it, as the situation did not arise in the Buddha's time to talk about informational privacy and data protection.

Group Privacy

Another advantage of the Buddhist conception proposed here is that it makes better sense of the emerging concept of group privacy. Basically this is privacy of a group of individuals rather than of single ones. Group privacy needs to be protected when there is sensitive information shared by a group such that the group could be harmed if someone from the outside gained access to the information. For example, an ethnic group might share some genetic information together which is distinctive to them and which is a marker for some special health condition. Thus the group tends to be vulnerable to discrimination because of their specific condition, especially if the group is also poor and powerless. Health insurance companies might be reluctant to insure the group at the same price as others because of their increased risks. So instead of protecting the privacy of each individual, in this case it is more appropriate and practical to protect the privacy of the whole group, treating the group as if they were one individual unit.

The idea of group privacy is not new. Recently Luciano Floridi also discusses the notion, and usefully provides a metaphysical account of the notion.[14] According to Floridi, "We need to be more inclusive because we are underestimating the risks involved in opening anonymised personal data to public use, in cases in which *groups* of people may still be easily identified and targeted."[15] Stephen Karanja provides a userful account of the notion, referring specifically to marginalized groups.[16] He also gives a rather detailed survey of the literature in the field, which is growing, but still the literature is dominated by those who emphasize exclusively the individual notion of privacy. Moreover, Chandran Kukanthas also talks about the closely related notion of "cultural privacy"[17] which he partially defends. Bloustein treats the whole notion of group privacy in his book, and he argues basically links the concept up with that of human dignity, as he contends that group privacy is an extension of individual privacy, which is based on dignity.[18] However, these scholars seem to base their theory of group or cultural privacy on the individual. Kukanthas, for example, makes it clear that the reason why cultural privacy should be protected in some form is that it is ultimately the autonomy and

---

[14]Floridi (2014).

[15]Floridi, "Open Data," p. 2.

[16]Karanja (2008).

[17]Kukanthas (2008).

[18]Bloustein (2004).

dignity of the persons within a cultural group that need to be protected.[19] This reliance on the individuals is natural for those who believe that privacy can only be justified through reference to individual autonomy and dignity which is part of the liberal theory of privacy, to which I am offering a more defensible alternative.[20]

The Buddhist account appears to do a better job, I believe, at accounting for group privacy because it is not based on the idea of an autonomous, self-subsisting individual, but on a pragmatic consideration of how protection of privacy promotes the values that society believe to be valuable and need to be cherished and protected. The metaphysical assumption of the Buddhist account also seems to be more streamlined. As we have seen, Buddhist philosophy regards the individual person as ultimately composed of more basic elements, which makes it rather easy to step from the making up of an individual through more basic elements to the making up of a social group through individual persons. Of course there are differences in the two steps, such as the individual person can move his or her body together as one unit, but the social group is not glued together in the same way, and so on. But the basic idea is roughly the same—things are composed of more basic elements and what tie them together are causes and conditions, which mean that no entity can remain the same throughout since everything always depends for their being on other things. So instead of grounding group or cultural privacy on the privacy or autonomy of individuals, the Buddhist notion would propose that group privacy is grounded on the instrumental or pragmatic value of protecting the privacy of the group instead. As long as the group is recognized as existing, then the privacy of the group can be recognized and protected accordingly. Here we need to refer to some concrete examples. Bloustein's favorite examples of group privacy are lovers and the football huddle.[21] In both cases the lovers and the football players share some intimate information together which they do not want others to know. Lovers share intimate secrets known only to themselves; the football players in a huddle share closely guarded secrets about their plan for the next play. However, the privacy of these groups are contingent upon the existence of the groups themselves, and this is nothing mysterious. Lovers can tire of each other and go their separate ways; football players quit playing together and also go their separate ways. In these cases the group no longer exists, so the privacy of these groups depends on the contingent condition that exists only for a period of time and the privacy also depends on what kind of information the group feels needs to be protected. It is not a matter of there being something that is ontologically over and above the individuals. The Buddhist notion does not imply that individuals have no rights or dignity; on the contrary, individuals can have all the rights and dignity they are entitled to have, but those

[19]Chandran Kukanthas, "Cultural Privacy," p. 78.

[20]Here Nissenbaum's notion of contextual integrity in *Privacy in Context* is still very much relevant, and is in fact another alternative. It can also be seen that what I am doing here is to flesh out Nissenbaum's framework; that is, group privacy can be seen as an aspect of privacy considerations requiring a different set of norms, in other words one of the contexts in which privacy is given importance.

[21]Edward J. Bloustein, *Individual & Group Privacy*, p. 125.

rights and dignity are derived from the presuppositions and requirements of a liberal democratic society rather than from their metaphysical status. Furthermore, the privacy of a group does not have to be derived from the dignity of each individual, but the group itself needs to protect some information as part of their functioning as a group, such as lovers or a football team.

However, a more serious criticism of the notion of group rights comes from thinkers who believe that the notion may lead to giving priority to the group rather than to its individual members. Comparing the notions of group privacy and group rights, Karanja says, "... the notion of group rights, like minority rights, has come under attack from liberal theorists as a negation of the concept of universality of rights. Group rights are inherently group differentiation and thus the exact opposite of universalism." [22] The fear is that when privacy rights are tied to groups, then this leads to differentiation of groups and to rights being tied up to only specific groups. However, in the case of privacy rights, I do not see anything seriously wrong in this. Lovers share their secrets, their private memories together and these secrets and memories deserve to be protected as part of the shared connection that the lovers have toward each other. Different lovers certainly have different stories and memories, and these memories deserve to be protected too. Thus it is not the content of the secrets of each lover group that is universal; this cannot be. But it is the fact that each lover group, and all other kinds of group for that matter, has privacy rights when they have information that they wish to keep only among the members of the group. Thus group privacy as a right is different from minority rights in this regard. Another fear is that group rights or group privacy might lead to giving priority to the group rather than to particular individuals. This is the standard group versus individual fear, which arises usually when the group is regarded as an ontologically objective entity appearing more powerful than each individual within it. For example, the group may decide that a particular piece of information is private to the group and forbids each member to divulge it to the outside world, but some members of the group might feel oppressed by this. Critics of the notion of group privacy might use this kind of example to point out that group privacy, as is possibly the case with group rights, gives priority to the collective rather than the individual, and hence is unethical. When we view the whole issue under the lens of the autonomous individual theory of privacy, then it is understandable why such a criticism could arise. However, under the pragmatic approach, the oppression of the collective over the individual can only happen when some members in the group use force to coerce others into following their orders. When the "group" tells its members that certain information is "private" and not to be divulged, there is an imbalance of power going on, as the members do not have the same power as the leader of the group. Thus in fact the information in question is actually private only to the leader only, and it is highly tenuous to hold that the information is part of privacy of the group. Group privacy should apply to the information that all members of the group commonly feel that it needs to be kept inside the group, and

[22]Stephen Kabera Karanja, "Privacy and Protection of Marginalized Social Groups," p. 9.

not to information that the powerful leader tells his followers not to tell to anyone outside. If this is the case, then the latter case should not be considered a case of group privacy at all.

Privacy and Universal Value

The review of research findings on privacy from Thailand, China, Japan and Africa that we have seen in the last chapter show a richness and diversity of how privacy is conceptualized and understood by these cultures. It is perhaps only natural that the argument whether privacy is universal or not emerges out of the authors' conviction on the issue in the first place. That is, there is a good chance that if the authors' actually believe that privacy is a universal value that is valid across cultures, their arguments through surveying what a particular culture (be it Chinese or Japanese, or any other) would have to say on the issue would then support their argument. But perhaps this is a gratuitous way of looking at things. Nonetheless, what is clear is that there is a diversity even among scholars coming from the same culture about whether privacy is universal or not. This shows that the question is a very important and complicated one.

Let us take a look back at the paper by Orito and Murata in the last chapter.[23] The paper has generated a response by Göran Collste, who argues that the concept of privacy is a universal one.[24] According to Collste, "privacy is a vague concept and it is not possible to identify one Western view of privacy and—for example—the Japanese views of privacy."[25] Here Collste's main argument relies on the notion that individual autonomy, i.e., one's construction of an "I" functioning as a fulcrum point, is a necessary condition for privacy. Since every person in every culture is an individual, so the argument goes, the right to privacy is thus innate in all individuals, no matter what culture they happen to belong to. Collste is careful in pointing out that different cultures may have different opinions on which information should be regarded as private, but ultimately they are not in disagreement as to privacy is a value or not.[26]

Let us call this type of argument that relies on the metaphysical conception of the individual ego, the "metaphysical argument" for privacy. In fact we have seen this type of argument before in the previous chapter. The idea is that privacy is part and parcel of an individual person. The very fact that there is an individual person who is autonomous, capable of thinking by oneself, and so on, presupposes that there be

---

[23]Yohko Orito and Kiyoshi Murata, "Privacy Protection in Japan: Cultural Influence on the Universal Value," available at http://www.kisc.meiji.ac.jp/~ethicj/Privacy%20protection%20in%20Japan.pdf (retrieved July 8, 2015).

[24]Collste (2008).

[25]Göran Collste, "Global ICT-ethics," p. 76.

[26]Göran Collste, "Global ICT-ethics," pp. 80–81.

a certain form of privacy that sets up a kind of boundary line between oneself and everything outside. The boundary then defines the individual's private sphere. Viewed this way privacy is thus universal because obviously every culture does consist of individuals. Collste then points out that one should not confuse privacy as a universal value in this regard with the kind of information each culture deems to be "private." Hence Muslim cultures may regard the woman's hair as private, since it proscribes rules to protect the woman's hair to be seen in public, whereas in the West or in other Asian cultures this is not an issue. This does not show, according to Collste, that privacy is not a value for the Muslims. On the contrary, the very opposite is the case because the woman's hair is a very private issue and only the husband and the immediately family members of the woman can see her hair. Westerners are typically reluctant to share personal information such as one's income, family issues and so on to a stranger or an acquaintance, whereas in China this is quite common place. This also does not show that either culture does not have the concept of privacy.

However, Collste's argument misses the point when it argues that privacy is universal because it is presupposed by the individual ego. For Collste's argument to work, the individual ego must be metaphysically there as a self-subsisting entity. But as we have seen from this is very much a contested issue. For the argument proposed by Collste to work, the individual ego must be there as a distinct ontological entity, and arguments from the Buddhist tradition have shown that this is not the case, as the individual ego appears to be a construction, albeit a very persistent one.

Basically, my difference from Collste on the question of the universality of privacy is that, while Collste believes that privacy as a normative value is universal because it is based on the autonomy and dignity of the individual person, I take a rather different stance of basing privacy on the question whether privacy does bring about the desired goals and values, in this case democratic ones and one where the individual is given respect, dignity and autonomy. Giving individuals respect, autonomy and dignity are crucial and indispensable for a functioning democratic society and at the global level this is required as well because norms have to be universalized to facilitate globalization. These global norms, of which privacy is a part, cannot function at all if some country in the globalized arena refuses to participate. This will create disruptions that could bring the whole process down. Thus there is an interest in seeing that norms and guidelines are largely the same throughout. This does not have to be based on the metaphysical assumptions of liberalism.

It has to be noted that, even though privacy is ultimately not a universal value, this does not mean that it is a culture specific value either. Here the model proposed by Mizutani, and others is most relevant.[27] On the one hand, cultures share certain minimal level of beliefs and practices. Collste is indeed right when he claims that Japanese culture does value the fact that certain information should be kept

[27]Mizutani et al. (2004).

confidential as much as the West does. However, when it comes to the question of what kind of information should be kept secret, there can well be divergences in practices. The extreme example of the Roman latrine alluded to earlier in the previous chapter shows that the Romans had a very different understanding of what is private than we do. But that does not mean that the Romans did not have the concept of privacy at all, for even Romans had to maintain some space around an individual so as to demarcate him or her as an individual person. Hence beyond the minimal level there is what Mizutani and others call the "rich" level where there are the traditions and stories behind certain concepts. There being the distinction between these two levels does not imply that privacy is totally a culture specific concept. Nor does it imply that relativism in value theory is a tenable position. Here Ess's view on ethical pluralism is also directly relevant, as it charts a middle course between universalism on the one hand and particularism on the other.[28]

Collste tries to argue that privacy is a universal concept by arguing at the metalevel, claiming that moral universalism is a tenable position. Since moral universalism is tenable, so the argument goes, privacy is a universal concept because privacy is justified through moral universalism (such as privacy is presupposed for an individual). Here one needs to be very careful in not conflating issues that look very similar but definitely are not the same. It is an empirical fact that different cultures and different historical periods had different understandings of what is private. But the moral relativist regarding privacy would go a step further and claim that privacy can only be justified through reliance on the actual belief of certain culture and there is no possible of justifying the moral value of privacy across cultures. Basing his argument on the metaphysical underpinning of the autonomous status of an individual person, Collste then argues that privacy, since it is presupposed by such underpinning, is thus universal. At one level, there is no question of justifying privacy, since the emphasis is on the descriptive task of saying what the attitudes of certain cultures are regarding privacy. But Collste then makes a universalist moral argument, claiming in effect that privacy is justified because it is presupposed by individual autonomy, as we have seen. According to the pragmatist, on the other hand, what is at issue here, supposing that the pragmatist accepts the cogency of the argument from individual autonomy, is not so much on critiquing the argumentative move from autonomy to justification of privacy, as on critiquing the very idea of individual autonomy itself. For the pragmatist, even the concept of individual autonomy is culture specific, and thus one cannot claim it to be universal.

In fact even in the West there are divergences as to how privacy should be understood and justified. De Boni and Prigmore point out that the usual conception of privacy appearing in legislation is Anglo-Saxon and empiricist in its philosophical orientation, and that other philosophical traditions all have a claim to truth,

[28]Charles Ess develops his view on ethical pluralism in many places. See, for example, "Ethical Pluralism and Global Information Ethics," *Ethics and Information Technology* 8(2006): 215–226. A comprehensive textbook on the topic and on others is his *Digital Media Ethics*, 2nd Edition (Cambridge: Polity Press, 2014).

and that one viewpoint should not have precedence over others in this regard.[29] Taken literally, this is a straightforward relativistic position, but perhaps what De Boni and Prigmore are getting at is that the usual conception of privacy that is prevalent in the law and in academic literature is a product on one culture and one philosophical tradition only; hence the implication is that, since other philosophical traditions at least have an equal claim to validity, privacy according to these other traditions should be given consideration too. In the end, the result of these considerations of privacy in various cultures might turn out to be practically and largely the same, but it may not. In the case that it may not, De Boni and Prigmore would presumably argue that the divergent conceptions of privacy should live together side by side, or they might go one step further and search for an underlying common ground.

In fact the presupposition of De Boni and Prigmore is too broad. Dan Burk shows that there is a divergence of viewpoints on how privacy should be conceptualized and justified between the US and the European Union, where the former prefers a consequentialist one of justifying privacy through its utilities and other desirable goals, and the EU pays more attention to the right of people in having their privacy protected.[30] Hence the EU prefers the deontological or right-based theory to the consequentialist one. This philosophical difference led to a number of concrete divergences in laws and regulations on privacy in the two continents. What Burk has shown, in effect, is that we cannot talk about the West as a monolithic entity. Both the two theories, the consequentialist and the deontological theories, are both well supported by numerous works in ethics and philosophy, and neither can be singled out to represent the Western philosophical position regarding privacy as a whole. This divergence may support De Boni and Prigmore's relativistic stance. Since there are divergences, they should be recognized and more importantly the dominant conception should be recognized as belonging to just one position among others only. But the fact that there are many competing ethical theories does not by itself imply that any theory is as good as any other. The fact that the dominant conception (which could well be either the US or the EU position) belongs to one cultural tradition does not necessarily imply that all other conceptions belonging to other cultural traditions are valid. Otherwise no philosophical enterprise of trying to construct arguments to convince others would be pointless.

In any case, this is a clearly philosophical enterprise. Given that the outcomes of the situation where difference cultures entertain significantly divergent conceptions of privacy would be less palatable than otherwise, it would be desirable to search for a common goal that would tie up all these divergent conceptions together. Fortunately, we have seen from the scholarly works that discuss privacy according

---

[29]Marco De Boni and Martyn Prigmore, "Cultural Aspects of Internet Privacy," available at http://citeseerx.ist.psu.edu/viewdoc/download?doi=10.1.1.14.6032&rep=rep1&type=pdf (retrieved July 8, 2015).

[30]Burk (2008).

to the various Asian cultures that such a common notion of privacy could be found, even if the cultural milieux wherein such a notion exists are totally different. But these works discussing the Asian conceptions did not go as far as stating explicitly which kind of supposedly universal conception of privacy should be preferred, namely those belonging to the deontological or the consequentialist camp, or more concretely the US or the EU way of justifying and regulating privacy. If it is the case that the existence of different ethical theories does not lead to ethical relativism, then we do have reasons to prefer one theory over the other. Thus there should be, and in fact there are, arguments that should be able to convince sufficiently reasonable people to see the advantages of one theory over others. In the same vein, the fact that there are cultural differences in how privacy should be understood and justified does not imply relativism either, though one can obviously argue for one position, or the position of one culture, over the others.

So there seem to be a dilemma. Taking the cue from Burk, if we accept that the differences between the positions of the US and the EU are irreconcilable, then we seem to get started on the very slippery slope toward relativism. On the other hand, we certainly to do not want to impose the viewpoint of one culture over all others, like the European colonial rules did toward their subjects in the past. This is a very difficult issue. However, the issue is further complicated by the fact that in the case of the US and the EU the differences work on two levels at the same time, namely the first-order level of which rules and regulations regarding privacy should prevail, and the second-order one of justifying those rules and regulations through philosophical theory. In order to unpack all these tangles, let us focus ourselves on one particular example of privacy protection, that of a regulation of protection of personal data.

It is rather well known that the European Union has perhaps the strongest law against violation of personal data in the world. This stems from the Europeans' belief in fundamental human right, which cannot be violated and which is the duty of governments to protect. The US, on the other hand, tends to view privacy more in utilitarian terms. Especially after the passing of the Patriot Act as a result of the September 11, 2001 attach, US authorities seek to enhance security, even though in doing so privacy could be compromised.[31] Movius and Krup argue that laws and regulations in each country are influenced by the countries' particular traditions, histories, values and so on; thus divergences are to be expected.

Nonetheless, in discussing the divergencies in the rules and regulations about privacy in various countries, we need to see how much different these norms are from one another as well as how similar they really are. In any comparison between two things, there will always be both differences and similarities, and when there are differences one can always see how much the two things are different and in what aspects. Thus, in saying that privacy norms in two countries, for example, are different, it is possible that the different aspects are emphasized, neglecting for the time being the similar ones. Hence, in saying that the privacy norms are different in

---

[31]Movius and Krup (2009).

the US and the EU, perhaps those who say this overlook the obvious similarities, such as, for example, privacy should be protected to a certain extent. The point of this is that, in philosophical discussion of universalism versus particularism, too often the emphasis is put on the dichotomous relation between the two. If common traits can be found in the diverse cultures, then this might give support to universalism. On the other hand, if no common trait can be found, then particularism or relativism might be justified. Of course we should not confuse between the empirical description of cultures and the normative assessment of what should be the right way of making normative judgments. But quite often we see that arguments for either universalism or particularism rely on these empirical descriptions.

Thus although the privacy norms between the US and the EU are different, one cannot deny that there are consideration amount of similarities. This point alone shows that arguments purporting to derive the conclusion that privacy norms are relativistic from the mere fact of cultural differences are untenable, because there are always both differences and similarities in the cultures. Moreover, this also shows that differences or similarities between cultures are perhaps a matter of choice—it depends on whether one chooses to look at either differences or similarities. But if this is the case, then the whole debate between moral universalism and moral particularism tends to break down, because the differences and similarities that give rise to this normative debate are a matter of where to look rather than of objectively existing in themselves.[32]

In order to see this more clearly, let us have a closer look at the argument. The differences between the US and the EU on privacy issues are focused more on how privacy should be justified rather than on what actually constitutes privacy. Thus, both Europeans and Americans obviously agree that peeking into someone's house is a violation of the houseowner's privacy. The difference between the two, presumably, is that the American typically refers more to consequentialist reasoning whereas her European counterpart tends to resort more to individual rights. On the one hand, one can push for a relativistic argument saying that there can be no absolutely correct judgment as to whether the right-based or the consequentialist theory is the one true theory, basing the argument on the fact that there is a disagreement on this. On the other hand, one can also use the same fact to conclude that moral judgments must converge toward one true position, since both the Americans and the Europeans agree on what counts as privacy. The issue seems to be based on where one looks and where one finds the similarities or the differences.

One can certainly extrapolate this argument to cover the case of differences between the West and the East, for example. One of the main differences, as we have seen, is that the West tends to be more individualistic whereas the East more

[32]The issue here is quite similar to the debate on "Asian bioethics" in bioethics literature. Some bioethicists have proposed that there be Asian bioethics which is distinct from Western one, arguing that there are many differences in normative judgments and ways of justification between East and West. However, this position has been criticized as relativistic; these scholars point out, on the contrary, that there are significant common elements in bioethical judgment systems in the East and West. For more detail see Hongladarom (2008).

community based. This is a stereotype of course, but at least it suffices to make the point. We have seen that people in the Eastern cultures do not typically regard matters such as one's personal income or one's family background and history as being private. Westerners, on the other hand, would tend to view these matters as belonging to their personal, private, domain which is not easily divulged to strangers. Thus an Easterner might be less reluctant to tell this kind of information to strangers than a Westerner. This is a first-order level of the issue, where the difference lies at how privacy is perceived. If one focuses on this, then one might have a basis for a kind of relativistic argument. However, if one focuses instead on the commonality, such as on the shared understanding of the private as opposed to the public (even though what counts as either might be different), then one has a basis for a more universalistic argument. Again, following ethical pluralism developed by Ess, whether we should view privacy, or in fact any issues in normative judgment of this kind, depends much on where we choose to look.[33]

So does this mean that privacy is a universal value? There is no simple answer to this question if what I have argued so far is tenable. One has to supply further information such as at what level the privacy mentioned in the question is actually located. At one level, the privacy may be clearly divergent, but at another, more abstract level, the divergent cultural judgments can certainly converge. In fact the Buddhist and pragmatic conception can help explicate the situation quite clearly. Once we do not think that there is a philosophical truth to be found regarding whether which system of value or which cultural system is the true one, then we are free to focus on whether those systems are effective in bringing about desired goals or not. In the case of privacy, today's globalized world is such that it is very difficult, if not impossible, for a country to remain isolated and to engage with the global community would mean that the country has to accept certain norms, which include protection of privacy rights. What the Buddhist conception shows us is the possibility that different cultures may share the same norms, but the languages in which those norms are couched and the way they are justified can be different. For example, Thai and European cultures may share the same norms on privacy as both belong to the global community. However, Thai culture might decide to ground the talks of privacy in Buddhist language, as I am doing in this book, while the Europeans ground their conception of privacy in the usual, Western way. As long as the resulting conception is acceptable to both sides when they work with each other closely in the global arena, there does not seem to be anything wrong with that. Although Thai culture decides to couch the language of privacy under the traditional context of Buddhism, but if the protection of privacy rights of individuals and their groups are as effective as those who justify their privacy rights on the autonomy and dignity of individuals, then I do not see why the Thais should not continue with their policy.

[33]Ess (2006, 2014).

This way of justifying a value through indigenous cultural system may be similar to Rawls' proposal of the "overlapping consensus"[34] in political liberalism where those who participate in the townhall meeting set aside their metaphysical or religious beliefs in order to participate with their peer only in political terms.[35] My proposal, on the other hand, does not advocate that participants leave their metaphysical beliefs behind; on the contrary, they should fully espouse them and share them with their peer in the global arena so that each culture can learn from each other. (One purpose of this present book is to do just that, sharing insights gleaned from Buddhist to the international scholarly community.) It is to show that each culture has a resource which can lead to commonalities or topics for common deliberations. If my Buddhist theory of privacy is tenable, then this can contribute quite a great deal to the global concern in information ethics without getting mired in the fruitless debate over universalism or relativism.

Conclusion

We have seen that privacy is not something that can be based on an atomic conception of the individual person, for according to the Buddhist-based interpretation that I am proposing there is no such metaphysical basis. We have also seen that Buddhist philosophy provides a number of useful insights into how this can actually be done. One can have a way of justifying privacy as well as a complete conception of the concept without relying on the metaphysical belief in the individual subject. Furthermore the Buddhist conception also gives us a novel and useful way of understanding group privacy. The mainstream view that such a metaphysical conception is needed as a foundation for right and autonomy is found to be ultimately untenable because it is possible for us to have a system of right and autonomy which is based on a pragmatic consideration, such as the notion that right and autonomy of conventionally individual subject are necessary in order to achieve certain desired goals such as a fully democratic polity. As rights and autonomy are safeguards against abuse of power, and as privacy functions prominently in such a system, privacy then is crucial as an integral part of any attempt to curb abuse of power by the authorities. Buddhism, with its elaborate view on the nature of the individual and how reality is constituted, provides a fertile ground for this alternative conception of privacy and how it is justified.

One might object, however, why an elaborate system of justification of privacy is needed. Why, one might ask, do we need to bother with Buddhism and the critique of the metaphysical status of the individual in discussing privacy? One possible answer is because one *can* certainly justify privacy on pragmatic or

[34]I have developed the idea that Rawls' view on political liberalism could be used as a basis for intercultural dialog. See Hongladarom (2004). See also Ess (2007).
[35]See Rawls (2005).

instrumental grounds. One can certainly argue that privacy right is needed as a bulwark against unjust power wielded by the authorities, saying that it is our desired goal to have certain amount of autonomy and space within which we can operate freely without being subject to constant scrutiny by others. The whole idea hinges on the *desirability* of having such a space. However, when one is pressed to come up with an answer as to why the pragmatic conception is superior to the usual conception of relying on the metaphysical view of the individual person, one is then forced to come up with a philosophical system of one's own as an alternative to the mainstream conception. Thus, when one is asked why bother with the Buddhist or the pragmatic approach, which sounds philosophical and which does not seem to relate directly on the day to day issue of privacy protection, an answer is that if there is no need to come with such elaborate justificatory or philosophical argumentation, then one does not have to do that at all. Nonetheless, philosophy comes up to the fore when there is a need for it, and here the need does come when the usual system of how privacy is justified appears to be rather inflexible in dealing with intercultural issues that we have seen throughout the book. One problem is that the usual way of justifying privacy, one that relies on the atomic, self-subsisting individual, is found only in the West and does not ring a bell when privacy issues are transplanted in the non-Western cultures. If there is a way of justifying privacy that does all the work but is more resonant with the traditions of the non-Western culture, then it seems that is a reason for preferring the conception proposed here.

Furthermore, I have tried to argue that the pragmatic conception proposed here can well stand on its own and does not actually depend on the fact that it belongs to the East or other non-Western cultures. That is, the pragmatic conception has its own merits which even the West should adopt. One of the merits is that the pragmatic conception does a better job when there are differences in how privacy is conceptualized and how this is spelled out in actual practices, such as in formulation of actual regulations. The difference within the West between the US and the EU regarding how privacy issues should be justified is a clear case in point. Both the US and the EU belong to the Western culture, but there are significant differences between the two, as we have seen in Chap. 2. As the mainstream conception is more rigid, it is less amenable to reconciling the differences between the two than the proposed, pragmatic conception. Furthermore, relying on the belief in intrinsic individual rights appear to chime more with the EU's position than that of the US. Nonetheless, the proposed conception is not the same as the consequentialism preferred by the US either, because consequentialism still presupposes the existence of individual persons as a metaphysical entity, something which our conception here rejects.

Not only can the Buddhist conception (which works as the basis of the pragmatic one) stand on its own philosophically speaking, the conception also does provide a novel way of accounting for the concept of group privacy. Since the conception does not rely on the existence of self-subsisting individual subject, making sense of group privacy is thus easier. The holder of privacy—the one whose information is to be protected—could be an individual or a group of individuals. There is no difference between the two as to how privacy can be attached. The liberal approach has a harder time because it has to reduce group privacy into privacy or autonomous rights of individuals comprising the group, thus for the liberal approach group privacy is always secondary. The Buddhist approach, on the contrary, makes it possible that group privacy and individual privacy are at the same level conceptually speaking. This is important, I believe, because group privacy has become a very important concept especially as the technologies of Big Data and Internet of Things are becoming more widespread. As Big Data manipulate data obtained from a very large number of individuals, we need a way to conceptualize privacy of these individuals as one entity rather than as single individuals banded together. Thus the Buddhist theory is useful not only for Thai people who need it as a source of insights for their construction of a theory, but the whole world can benefit from its distinctive and unique characteristics.

References

Bloustein eJ (2004) Individual & Group Privacy, 2nd edn. Transaction Publishers, New Brunswick, p 125

Burk D (2008) Privacy in the US and the EU. In: Hongladarom S, Ess C (eds) Information technology ethics: cultural perspectives. IGI Global, Hershey

Collste Göran (2008) Global ICT-ethics: the case of privacy. J Inf Commun Soc 6(1):76–87

Debatin B (2011) Ethics, privacy and self-restraint in social networking. In: Trepte S, Reinecke L (eds) Privacy online: perspectives on privacy and self-disclosure in the social web. Springer, Berlin, pp 47–60

DeCew J (1986) The scope of privacy in law and ethics. Law Philos 5:145–173

Ess C (2006) Ethical pluralism and global information ethics. Ethics Inf Technol 8:215–226

Ess C (2007) Cybernetic pluralism in an emerging global information and computing ethics. Int Rev Inf Ethics 7(2007). Available at http://www.i-r-i-e.net/inhalt/007/11-ess.pdf. Retrieved October 1, 2015

Ess C (2014) Digital media ethics, 2nd edn. Polity Press, Cambridge

Floridi L (2014) Open data, data protection, and group privacy. Philos Technol 27:1–3. doi:10.1007/s13347-014-0157-8

Hongladarom S (2004) Asian bioethics: what is it? Is there such a thing? Eubios J Asian Int Bioeth 14:194–197

Hongladarom S (2007) Analysis and justification of privacy from a Buddhist perspective. In: Hongladarom S, Ess C (eds) Information technology ethics: cultural perspectives. Idea Group Reference, Hershey, pp 108–122

Hongladarom S (2008) Universalism and particularism in the Asian bioethics debate. Asian Bioeth Review 1–14 (Inaugural Edition)

Karanja SK (2008) Privacy and protection of marginalized social groups. Stud Ethics Law Technol 2(3):1–22

Kukanthas C (2008) Cultural privacy. The Monist 91(1):68–80

Mackenzie C (2008) Relational autonomy, normative authority and perfectionism. J Soc Philos 39 (4):512–533

Mizutani M, Dorsey J, Moor JH (2004) The Internet and Japanese conception of privacy. Ethics Inf Technol 6:121–128

Movius LB, Krup N (2009) U. S. and EU privacy policy: comparison of regulatory approaches. Int J Commun 3:169–187

Nissenbaum H (2009) Privacy in context: technology, policy and the integrity of social life. Stanford University Press, Palo Alto

Rachels J (1975) Why privacy is important. Philos Public Aff 4(4):323–333

Rawls J (2005) Political liberalism. Columbia University Press, New York (expanded edition)

Regan P (1995) Legislating privacy: technology, social values, and public policy. University of North Carolina Press, Chapel Hill

Schulman M (2000) Little brother is watching you. In: Baird RM, Ramsower R, Robenbaum SE (eds) Cyberethics: social & moral issues in the computer age. Prometheus Books, Amherst, pp. 155–161

Sutt M (1995) The long discourses of the Buddha: a translation of the Dĩgha Nikāya. (trans Walshe M). Wisdom, Boston, pp 143–148 (for the English translation, and "Mahāli Sutta," available at http://84000.org/tipitaka/pitaka_item/v.php?B=9&A=4399&Z=4960 for the Thai translation)

Veltman A (2014) Autonomy and oppression at work. In: Veltman A, Piper M (eds) Autonomy, oppression and gender. OUP, Oxford, pp 280–300

Veltman A, Piper M (2014) Introduction. In: Veltman A, Piper M (eds) Autonomy, oppression and gender. OUP, Oxford, pp 1–11

Westlund A (2009) Rethinking relational autonomy. Hypatia 24(4):26–49

Index

S. Hongladarom, *A Buddhist Theory of Privacy*,
SpringerBriefs in Philosophy, DOI 10.1007/978-981-10-0317-2